2,10

SETON HALL UNIVERSITY
BX1758.2 .G513   SEMINARY
Christ & moral theology,

3 3073 00097669 4

D1074773

DARLINGTON SEMINARY LIBRARY
DARLINGTON, N. J. 07446

CHRIST

& MORAL THEOLOGY

BY LOUIS B. GILLON, O.P.

DARLINGTON SEMINARY LIBRARY
DARLINGTON, N. J. 07446

alba house
DIVISION OF THE SOCIETY OF ST. PAUL
STATEN ISLAND, N.Y. 10314

BX
1758.2.
B513

00456   c. 2

Original title: Cristo e la Teologia Morale, published by Edizioni Romane MAME

Translated by Cornelius Williams, O.P.

Nihil obstat: John A. Goodwine, J.C.D. — Censor Librorum

Imprimatur: ✠ Terence J. Cooke, D.D, V.G.
New York, N.Y., November 1, 1967

The Nihil obstat and Imprimatur are official declarations that a book or pamphlet is free of doctrinal or moral error. No implication is contained therein that those who have granted the Nihil obstat and Imprimatur agree with the contents, opinions or statements expressed.

Library of Congress Catalog Number: 66-17764

Designed, printed and bound in the U.S.A. by the Pauline Fathers and Brothers of the Society of St. Paul at Staten Island, New York as a part of their communications apostolate.

Copyright 1967 by the Society of St. Paul, 2187 Victory Blvd., Staten Island, N.Y. 10314

DARLINGTON SEMINARY LIBRARY

Contents

Contents

List of reviews quoted and their abbreviations

AHD   = Archives d'Histoire doctrinale et littéraire du Moyen-âge, Paris 1926 ff.

AER   = The American Ecclesiastical Review, Washington 1889 ff.

BGPTMA = Beiträge zur Geschichte de Philosophie (from vol. 27, 1828-30 onwards: und Theologie) des Mittelalters, Münster 1891 ff.

Bibl   = Biblica, Rome 1920 ff.

DenzS   = Enchiridion Symbolorum, Definitionum et Declarationum de rebus fidei et morum, first edited by H. Denzinger 1854, 32nd. edition by Adolf Schönmetzer, S.J. 1963.

EE   = Estudios ecclesiasticos, Madrid 1922-36, 1942 ff.

ITQ   = The Irish Theological Quarterly, Dublin 1864 ff.

MRS   = Mélanges de Science Religieuse, Lille 1944 ff.

NRT   = Nouvelle Revue Théologique, Tournai-Louvain-Paris 1879 ff.

PerRMCL = Periodica de re morali canonica liturgica, Rome 1912 ff.

RevSR   = Revue de Sciences Religieuses, Strassburg 1921 ff.

RPhL   = Revue philosophique de Louvain, Louvain, 1945 ff.

Sap   = Sapienza, Rome 1948 ff.

ThQ   = Theologische Quartalschrift, Tübingen 1819 ff, Stuttgart 1946 ff.

TiF   = Tijdschrift voor Filosofie, Louvain,

VInt   = La Vie Intellectuelle, Paris.

WW   = Wissenschaft und Weisheit, Düsseldorf 1934 ff.

Introduction

The well-known Belgian theologian, G.T. Bouquillon, has observed that moral theology today may be called "Alphonsian." It has taken its object, its methods and its spirit from the saintly Bishop of Naples. St. Alphonsus de Liguori himself has set down with perfect clarity the purpose he aimed at: *the formation of the Christian conscience*, which should in practice avoid the extremes of Laxism and of Rigorism. For the saintly Doctor it was a question of putting into the hands of his confreres a tool that would be of help to them in the ministry of the confessional and of preaching.

But the preaching of moral principles (what is to be done, what is to be avoided) is not the *whole* of preaching, which should also make known the Gospel message, dogmatic truths. On the other hand, the *Theologia Moralis* of St. Alphonsus is not *all* of moral theology, it does not exhaust all the possible forms of "moral theology."

It is evident that the *Theologia Moralis Alphonsiana* has but a limited scope. First of all, it does not attempt to describe the ways of union with God and the degrees of the spiritual life. And for all that the ways of divine union are of the greatest interest to the science that deals with human activity: are they not indeed its most perfect part, do they not constitute the most sublime point of human activity? Still less did St. Alphonsus wish to expound that vision of human action and destiny, that "Christian vision of the world," which many today expect of moral theology. It was thought then that all that pertained to ascetical theology on the one hand, and on the other to Apologetics or Christian philosophy. The moral theology of St. Alphonsus is, of set purpose, purely "practical," *ad usum confessariorum—for the use of Confessors.*

And still, moral theology taken integrally, cannot help knowing that human life has a goal, that this cannot be reduced to "the absurd." It has a meaning. Modern existentialists have at times called to mind the penetrating words which Shakespeare put into the mouth of Macbeth:

> Life's but a walking shadow, a poor player
> That struts and frets his hour upon the stage,
> And then is heard no more; it is a tale
> Told by an idiot, full of sound and fury,
> Signifying nothing.   (Act 5, Sc. 5, 24-28)

For the Christian, on the contrary, life signifies something, it has a meaning, which is God; it has a goal which is eternal life. Man arrives at this goal and tends towards this God who gives meaning to life in no other way than by a long series of acts, which, making use of his free-dom, he has the duty and the power of accomplishing each day. In this journey towards the absolute man must be aided by grace and enlightened by the law. The goal (finis ultimus, beatitudo) of human life, freedom, human activity, virtue and sin, law and grace: there we have discovered all the themes of the moral theology of St. Thomas. There is no contradiction between this vast theological "vision" of human activity and the theology of St. Alphonsus: the two can mutually complement one another.

*   *   *

St. Thomas is read by very few today and in that he shares the lot of great men of genius: Plato and Aristotle are no less neglected. "Moral theology" is in the dock of the accused; but the moral theology against which charges are brought in this "trial" is, it must be noted, rather the moral theology of the manuals which, as we mentioned already, take their inspiration in a greater or less degree from St. Alphonsus. But what is the reason for this "trial"? What is the meaning of this demand for a "new" moral theology? Some authors maintain that our moral theology is not "pious": there is no mention in it of Christ and the development of the spiritual life. With St. Bernard these critics want to find and feel here the name of Jesus: *when you unite, it means nothing to me, unless J read there of Jesus.* Besides, it is said, it is not the moral teaching which is preached to the devout Christian people, but rather a kind of "closed" moral teaching shut up in the confines of seminaries. It deals more with sins, censures etc., than with virtues, "conversion," than with growth in goodness which attains finally to union with God.

The easiest answer to this charge would be to say that moral theology is not *all* of theology: there is also ascetical and mystical theology, dogmatic and pastoral theology etc. We should not expect of moral theology what it never intended or wished to offer. The business of classical moral theology is to form *confessors*: and for that reason precisely there is question in it more of sins than of union with God, because divine union does not constitute "necessary" matter in the sacrament of Penance. And for all that the confessor must also know his dogmatic theology together with ascetical and mystical theology well. Neither St. Alphonsus nor any of the moralists ever doubted that.

What, then all this hubbub? Why this present bringing of moral theology to "trial"? The answer to this question is the object of this little book: taking into account, too, that moral theology is being blamed as well as everything else for not taking inspiration from the principles of modern philosophy, in a special way from the various personalist theories of today.

I Moral Theology
of "Personal Exemplarity"

Moral theology is commonly defined thus: the science of human actions in their relation to the final supernatural end of man, a science that operates under the double light of faith and reason.

Many today are of the opinion that the preceding description is incomplete. For it does in fact omit to emphasize the point that the moral life is the consequence of a "decision," of a total choice, by which *a personal subject takes up a position with regard to another person, takes up a radical attitude of acceptance or refusal. Either* the subject decides to take this other person as model and as pattern of his own life, willing in that case *to become a disciple*, to "follow" in all things the person who makes an urgent appeal to him: *come, follow me;* or, on the contrary, the subject remains in an attitude of *refusal*, it rejects the call that is made to him.[1]

That is, by and large, what the personalist philosophy means by "principle" of personal exemplarity, the term *principle* having here, as in Greek, the double meaning

---

1. Cf. F. TILLMANN, Die katholische Sittenlehre, III, Die Idee der Nachfolge Christi, Düsseldorf 1934, p. 44.

of absolute beginning and dominant force. It should be added as well that the terms used in latin languages (model, exemplar etc.) do not correspond entirely to the meaning of the German word *Vorbild*. For the "model" or "exemplar" call to mind immediately the idea of an object, of a *representation*, whether intellectual or sensitive; *Vorbild*, on the contrary, has nothing to do with the order of notional knowledge. It pertains more to the "order of the heart" than to that of "reason."

This person-model, which is for each one the focal point on which centers his whole "moral existence" can be *a great historical personality* of the past, a hero, a man of genius, a saint.[2] But just as there are positive and negative values, so too there are person-models characterized by a positive trait, others characterized by a negative feature. On the one hand we find love, on the other hate. Either it is a question of acting in the same manner as the person-model, or of doing everything that it does not do and of never doing what it does.

The moral teaching of "personal exemplarity" does not claim to suppress the norms of morality, moral and juridical laws. But these are abstract and general in character. They are meant to be placed and understood in

---

2. For Scheler the *Vorbild* is not necessarily a real, "historical" personality. Hamlet or Beatrice can, in his opinion, possess the traits or characteristics necessary for being a "person-model." Cf. M. SCHELER, *Vorbilder und Führer*, Nachlass I, Bern 1959, p. 259.

the context of the personal exemplar which gives to them concrete vitality: the *Vorbild* gives to the norms the life they lack.

The Christian will find in Christ the infinitely perfect exemplar of the moral life and at the same time the perfect conformity of a concrete life to that exemplar. Christ will be at one and the same time the supreme Norm, the Value, the Idea or Image and the Life.[3] As far as our moral theology is concerned, it is frequently satisfied with a code of abstract laws. It does not disengage itself sufficiently from the philosophical principle: that is good which is in harmony with "reason," and that is bad which is opposed to it. In preference to this abstract norm, which is a heritage from Aristotelianism, the following concrete norm will be set up: *all that is deemed good which is postulated by the development of the life of Christ in the moral activity of the Christian, and bad all that hinders it.*

Corresponding to the objective character of the person-exemplar (*Vorbild*) there is found, on the part of the subject, that decisive act by which it wishes *to become a disciple, to imitate* in all things the model. Here too where the term "imitation" is seen to be too weak, the German word *Nachfolge* has a much stronger meaning. In fact, it signifies precisely the act of "placing one-

---

3. F. TILLMANN, *op. cit.* p. 6.

self at the service of," of becoming a disciple and introduces us right away to the biblical perspectives of the
come, follow me.

In any event, the imitation of the model must not be
understood as a servile and impersonal *copying*. It is not
a question of reproducing materially the actions of the
Vorbild, but rather of acting "as" he would do in this
or that circumstance.[4] *To act as Christ would act in my
place* becomes thus the fundamental rule of Christian
Ethics.

There, then, is what moral theology really is. There
is no question of denying the usefulness of casuistry,[5] nor
of indulging in facile ironic criticism of the "moral teaching of the manuals." What Fritz Tillmann wants to
say, however, is this: that moral theology in the true
sense of the term, moral theology in the "fullest" sense
of that word, is to be found elsewhere. For it must consist in a global exposition of *the realities of the Christian
life* in their full context. It must no longer be aimed at a
strictly specialized audience, but must be directed towards the whole Christian people. It will be at one and
the same time both positive and speculative,[6] operating
under the light of Scripture and Tradition, in conformity
with the teaching of the Church.

---

4. *Ibid.*, p. 45.
5. *Ibid.*, p. 42.
6. *Ibid.*, p. 9.

It will, as a result, be simultaneously "Christian, biblical and spiritual." And for all that it will give to rational knowledge its due role. To deny that would be to go against the explicit teaching of St. Paul,[7] it would amount to refusing to admit that there exist in man certain moral exigences, certain "possibilities" of action, in fact a moral "nature" not destroyed by sin.[8] But a purely "immanent" moral teaching, which, having recourse to reason and sentiment alone, would claim to set up a *closed* world of values and norms, could on no account whatever have a place in the "Christian teaching on morals."[9]

Besides, such a moral teaching is in itself inadmissible, because it would fail to consider the real situation of man, which results from the two-fold fact of the fall and of redemption. It would, in fact, be dealing with man in the abstract, with man in the state of "pure nature." What, then, is to be the place of a rational ethics in moral theology? It occupies the same place in the context of moral theology as fundamental theology does in relation to dogmatic theology.[10] Fundamental theology is a *part* of theology; it is within the faith itself that it looks for the foundations of the faith.[11] It will be the same

---

7. *Rom.* 2, 14-15.
8. F. TILLMANN, *op. cit.* p. 15.
9. *Ibid.*, p. 18.
10. *Ibid.*, p. 27.
11. *Ibid.*, p. 27.

thing as *Vernunftethik*. It must not be an autonomous construction devoting its intention to a moral being taken in itself, situated outside and considered independently of divine Revelation and of the realities of the Christian life. On the contrary, it must show, with the aid of the light of faith, what man, considered concretely, is capable of realizing within the limits of the moral power which flows from his concrete nature, that same man whom grace has made the bearer of supernatural values.[12] Within the limits, then, of theology there is a place for a "rational ethics," but limited and circumscribed on all sides, because its subject of consideration belongs at one and the same time entirely to nature and to super-nature.[13] There is no question, then, of *prefacing* moral theology with this splendid edifice, purely rational in character, which we call "fundamental" moral theology.

*   *   *

The writings of THEODORE STEINBUCHEL (✝ 1949) present us with a more rigorous systematization of all this from the philosophical point of view. According to the professor of Tubingen, the moral life is not first and foremost the observance of a law, but rather the free

12. *Ibid.*, p. 22.
13. *Ibid.*

affirmation of an EGO in relation to a THOU. In the case of the Christian moral life we will find ourselves dealing with the answer of the human Ego to the call of God.[14] But the moral "life" and moral "science" are two quite different things. The latter presupposes a knowledge of the nature and structure of man, that he is not a pure essence, but essence and existence. The free realization of the possibilities of existence presupposes that man is *spirit* and *freedom*.[15] He is body, soul, spirit; not, however, a mere juxtaposition of these three elements, but *a whole* constituted by them.[16] Thus we have attained to the "person," which is a being in its own right, endowed with freedom and self-consciousness.[17] The person, however, is by no means to be identified with consciousness of self. Steinbuchel rejects pure actualism and maintains that the person is a *substance*.[18] Otherwise it would be impossible to explain the *permanence* of the Ego. But neither is the person in any way that inert mass, that "thing," which the term substance "evokes" for modern philosophy. In reality, the person is an essence which is defined and determined with ref-

---

14. T. STEINBUCHEL, *Religion und Moral im Lichte christlicher personaler Existenz*, Frankfort-M., 1951, p. 169.

15. T. STEINBUCHEL, *Die philosophische Grundlegung der katholischen Sittenlehre*, I, 1, Düsseldorf 1938, pp. 231-233.

16. *Ibid.*, p. 299.

17. T. STEINBUCHEL, *Religion und Moral*, p. 178.

18. *id.*, *Die philosophische Grundlegung*, p. 345.

erence to the accomplishment of its own acts (*Aktvoll-ziehendes Wesen*)—an expression which Sheinbuchel takes from the philosophy of Scheler.

Person and personality are two quite different things. The person is a reality of the "ontological" order, whereas the personality implies an axiological content, that is, it is rooted in the "ontical" order.[19] The personality is the person in so far as it has become the subject of "values." All that presupposes that the person is not at all something enclosed within itself, nor is it full developed at to all its possibilities. It can either perfect and complete itself or diminish and waste away. When it succeeds in becoming the subject of values it has become "personality."

How is this development of the personality brought about? Here it must be observed that the human person is not absolute transcendence situated in sublime isolation face to face with being. It finds its *limit* in the personality of the OTHER. The EGO is limited or circumscribed on all sides by the THOU. On top of this, the person includes at one and the same time a relation to the Other as its limit and a possibility of going beyond this limit.[20] The opposition will then become "communion" between one person and the other. In the last

---

19. *id., Religion und Moral*, p. 178. The terminology is taken from Heidegger, but the meaning is radically modified.
20. *Ibid.*, p. 178.

analysis, the being of the person is not the "monologue" of the absolute Spirit, as Hegel conceived it, but rather the "dialogue."[21] The relation to the other will be the "fundamental phenomenon" of the spiritual being.[22]

The person does not find itself confronted only with the other, with another individual person; it finds itself in the presence of a much vaster complex of things: family, nation, the entire universe, a complex of things which it has not created and which has an essential role in its own axiological development. Precisely here comes to light a capital difference of "situation" between Greece and Christianity. In Christianity man does not come to grips with an impersonal cosmos, but rather is he confronted with a God who is person. For the Christian the natural law is not the emanation of an impersonal *Logos,* as it was for the Stoic; but rather is it the *voice* of a personal God.[23]

God expects, then, from the Christian an *answer* which should imply for the Christian a "personal" determination, a "personal" decision. Only God can demand such an answer, not the laws of the cosmos, because

21. In the order of knowledge already this borderline situation, this *Grenzsituation,* makes itself apparent. The act of knowledge implies, with regard to the object known, an act of renunciation, a recognition of limit: things would appear as limiting the free activity of the Ego. But knowledge also implies a gift of self to the object. Cf. *Religion und Moral,* p. 180.

22. *Die philosophische Grundlegung,* p. 279.

23. *Religion und Moral,* p. 164.

only a person can bind or oblige another person.[24] One must go even further and reflect that the law as such cannot set up a personal relationship between God and man. Since the law is abstract and universal, the individual precept (*Gebot*) alone constitutes a truly complete exigence for the personal subject which finds itself in a concrete singular situation. The law must, in consequence, have become a *personal precept* if we are to be in a position to demand from the person that total gift of self, that consecration to God and to the neighbor, which is theological charity.[25] This insistence on the concrete and singular situation of the person is radically opposed to the moral teaching of Kant, which is *universalist*: act in such a manner that your action may be set up as a universal maxim. On the contrary, with Kierkegaard and Scheler, one should consider that the person can, when it is question of an obligation's content, be aware that it refers to him alone: act always as if you heard a divine call which refers to no-one but you.[26]

The danger that threatens the moralist, then, will be the "moralization" of moral teaching. Instead of concentrating on the individual concrete man, on the person in its own special situation *hic et nunc*, one will be

---

24. *Ibid.*, p. 167.
25. *Ibid.*, p. 169.
26. *Ibid.*

interested only in the working out of a code of abstract laws. The result of this will be that man precisely as conditioned by the living reality of his moral and religious experience will be lost sight of.[27]

*   *   *

The authors who for the past twenty years have drawn their inspiration from the moral theology of the *Nachfolge* have been above all interested in its religious and evangelical character. They have paid less attention to its philosophical roots. Let us examine some of the new elements which these have succeeded in adding to the synthesis of F. Tillmann and Th. Steinbuchel. Moral theology, it is maintained, must be elaborated in very close relationship to dogmatic theology, taking into account also the actual problems of Apologetics and the renewal of the spiritual life. In the last analysis it should not be anything more than a chapter, a part, of the theology of the Mystical Body.[28]

Our age is looking for a moral teaching that is authentically and totally Christian in character. In moral theology we must do away with that mass of casuistical solutions, with theoretical considerations, which lead the

27. *Ibid.*, p. 153.

28. T. SOIRON, *Das Christusgeheimnis und das christliche Leben*, WW 13 (1950) 99.

faithful to think that their moral existence is governed by quite another principle than the only valid one: *esse in Christo Jesu*. Christian existence has nothing to do with the "Greek" theory of the cardinal virtues, nor with a philosophical notion of law and conscience. Doubtless the Christian must recognize an order of duties which derive from the "natural" structures in which he finds himself involved: the family, the state, the universe. One can no longer be in ignorance of the fact that there exist moral values which the spiritual person as such, without the intervention of the light of faith, can perceive. But nothing of all that is "authentically" Christian. Besides, Christ is at one and the same time Lord of the cosmic order and of the order of grace. Nothing exists outside and independently of him. Everything is saved by adherence to him, all is lost without him. In the last analysis there is in moral theology but one sole norm, Christ himself, in whom all the precepts find their fulfillment.[29] In his commentary on *Matthew* 25, 31-46, Krautwig remarks that, on the day of judgment, the decisive thing will not be to have observed the precepts, nor to have had the virtues, nor to have expressed sublime thoughts about Christianity: the criterion will be *to have followed or not* the Master.[30] All this suffices to

---

29. N. KRAUTWIG, *Entfaltung der Herrlichkeit Christi. Eine Wesensbestimmung katholischer Moraltheologie*, WW 7 (1940) 85-86.
30. *Ibid.*

prove that the moral theology of the imitation of Christ (*Nachfolge Christi*) can in no way be satisfied with mere christological whitewashing (*if one forgive the expression*); it is in no wise a question of adding to the classical type of moral theology a veneer of something that will make it more attractive, or more "edifying." In reality there is here question of a radical "reform of structure." The intention is to substitute for a moral teaching that derives its inspiration from scholastic theology and its Aristotelian background a different moral theology, one that is wholly and authentically Christian.

The moral theology of the following of Christ (*Nachfolge Christi*) had a widespread repercussion in Germany, where it originated, in Belgium and in France.[31] In Italy,[32] on the contrary, in Spain[33] and in the Anglosaxon countries[34] it seems to make a lesser appeal. We should not, however, be surprised that the "moralists" in the classical sense of the term, should have reacted at

31. The following works may be noted: P. DELHAYE, *La théologie morale d'hier et d'aujourd'hui*, RevSR 27 (1953) 112-130; the collective work: *Morale chrétienne et reqûetes contemporaines*, Tournai-Paris, 1954; L. VEREECKE, *Histoire et Morale*, MSR 13 (1956) 5-18; S. PINCKAERS, *Renouveau de la théologie morale*, VInt Oct. 1956, 1-21. The essential ideas of Tillmann were the inspiration of B. HAERING'S manual, *Das Gesetz Christi*, Freiburg-B. 1954, translated into French, Italian and English.

32. Y. ZEILER, however, devoted part of his study to the matter up to 1935: *De conditione theologiae moralis hodierna*, PerRMCL 28 (1937) 117.

33. Cf. M. ZELBA, S.J., *Esposicion de la Moral cristiana*, EE 29 (1955) 65-80 (completely negative).

34. Some indications in W. CONWAY, *The science of Moral Theology. New Trends*, ITQ 22 (1955), 154-158.

times quite vigorously against a movement which not infrequently treated them in no way gently. Moral theology conceived in that fashion, remarked O. SCHILLING, is not in a position to "solve" the problems that face the moralist today. Schilling gives the example of sterilization, a problem then of great actuality in Germany. Is sterilization licit or not? In order to solve this problem is it sufficient to answer: "think as Christ would think in your place"? Would we not quite justifiably get the reply: and what would Christ decide precisely in such a case? We will find ourselves then obliged to have recourse to a reasoning process, to the famous reflex principles, in a word, to the "classical moral theology" so much discredited by the advocates of a "mystical" moral teaching.[35] The Following of Christ (Nachfolge Christi) is a very beautiful "Idea" (we shall see later the precise meaning of this term in idealistic philosophy); but, strictly speaking, it just cannot constitute that which we call the "principle" of moral theology, a principle from which may be drawn clear conclusions capable of guiding immediately and directly human activity. To put the matter briefly it can be said that Tillmann and his disciples have written a chapter of *biblical* theology but not a moral theology in the true sense of the term. This indeed cannot be satisfied with biblical data; it dare not neglect the teaching of the scholastics nor pass over un-

---

35. O. SCHILLING, *Das Prinzip de Moral*, ThQ 119 (1938) 422.

noticed the rich analyses of the casuists unless it wish to renounce completely its specific role. And here is another important criticism. The new moral theology excludes the classical "fundamental" moral teaching. It does, of course, make place for a Christian "anthropology" which will emerge automatically in the course of its elaborations. But the whole question of law it leaves to the jurist, and that of conscience to the psychologist. When all that has been cut away, can there still be any such thing as a true moral theology or does it not rather find itself unable to answer the questions, at times very fundamental ones, which are being put to it today?[36] And should this new moral theology, "biblical," "mystical" or what you like, in character, attempt to answer these questions, will it not be obliged to have recourse to the principles and methods and solutions of the old classical "moral theology"? And in that case the structure of the new moral teaching will be nothing more than a *veneer*, a kind of scenario, used to create a new appearance, on the traditional foundation of moral theology.

---

36. An account of these criticisms is to be found in P. HADROSSEK, *Die Bedeutung des Systemgedankes für die Moraltheologie in Deutschland seit der Thomas—Renaissance*, Munich 1950, pp. 329-332 also F. HUERTH, S.J., *Hodierna conscientiae problemata metaphysica, psychologica, theologica*, in the: Acts of the International Congress on the occasion of the 4th. centenary of the Pontifical University Gregoriana, I, Rome 1954, pp. 408-409: nihil obstat quominus in Ethica christiana exponenda . . . Christi vita . . . in centro ponatur, sed experientia et vita teste, neque fidelium institutio catechetica, neque efformatio futurorum sacerdotum neque ipsa scientifica . . . expositio Ethicae christianae contenta esse possunt illa formula: . . . *Quid faceret Christus si mei esset loco?*

II The New Movement in the Light of the History of Moral Theology

On account of their object and their method "dogmatic" and "moral" theology are considered by us today as two distinct sciences. However, the more one goes back in the past, the less clearcut appears this rigorous distinction. Let us listen to what Origen has to say. In the very first lines of his *De principiis*, the Alexandrian Master observes that those who believe that Christ is the Truth "cannot find anywhere else but in his words the *science* of the virtuous and of the blessed life."[1] The science of that which is to be believed is in no way separated from the science of the blessed life. And this latter business, which is, in the proper sense of the term, a "moral" preoccupation, is perhaps the more profound and the more fundamental one in Origen.

In the Middle Ages the number of authors who consider theology to be a "practical" science is great. The purpose and intention of theological wisdom, its very "sense" and meaning, is not limited to the order of pure knowledge for its own sake. Over and above and beyond the knowledge of the mysteries of the faith, theol-

---

1. ORIGEN, *De principiis*, Praef. ed. Koetschau, Leipzig 1913, p. 8.

ogy aims at making us virtuous, above all it aims at enkindling within us the affectivity and emotion, in a word, love of God *incendium amoris*.[2] Does not this essentially "practical" orientation of theology belong in reality to the domain of "moral" theology?

St. Thomas was not ignorant of the distinction between "dogmatic" and "moral" theology,[3] but he never for a moment thought of making *two* distinct sciences out of them. For him theology is *one* single science and essentially speculative, and still it extends its aim in the direction of human activity. It is by "extension" *practical*.

Obviously this unique theology, more affective in Bonaventure, in Thomas more intellectual, never pretended to meet all the needs of practical life. In the Middle Ages there was room beside it for the immense literature of the *Summae Confessorum*, the predecessors of our moral theology manuals.[4] These works did not aim at penetrating and examining deeply and scientifically theological *notions* or concepts (compare, for example, the treatise on lying as found in the *Summa Theologica* of St. Thomas and as found in the *Summa de casibus poenitentiae* of St. Raymond of Pennafort). These "notions" are rather *presupposed*. But a much larger place

---

2. St. Bonaventure, I Sent., Prol., q. 3, obj. 2.

3. St. Thomas, Quodlib. VII, a. 15; I, q. 1, a. 3, obj. 2.

4. An initial orientation in M. GRABMANN, *Storia della teologia cattolica*, pp. 189-205.

is given here to Canon Law than in the moral theology of the Doctors in Theology. One goes on right away to consider practical cases. In brief, the idea was to put into the hands of confessors an indispensable instrument for the exercising of their ministry.

In the first half of the 16th century the theologians are frequently both "speculative" and "casuistic" theollogians at one and the same time. Cajetan, Victoria, Banez, Suarez, these all develop, interminably at times, purely practical questions, even question of sheer casuistry. It is in the second half of the century that *specialization* makes its appearance and with it "moral theology" in the modern sense of the word. From now on "scholastic" theology withdraws into the domain of "dogmatic" theology. The new moral theology is distinguished from it not only as to scope and methods, which are a continuation and development of those proper to the medieval *Summulae*, but also as to *object*. For from now on the whole complex of man's moral activity becomes its special reserve, into which the "scholastic" theologians no longer dare to venture.[5]

In the 19th century in Germany a new moral the-

---

5. It is for that reason that the Carmelites of Salamanca (Salmanticenses) pass directly from the tract on charity to the tract on the states of life. More than 140 questions of the *Summa* of St. Thomas are left aside, and this omission is explained by the authors by saying that all this pertains to "moral" teaching rather than to "scholastic" theology. Was St. Thomas conscious of being a scholastic when writing the tract on prudence?

DARLINGTON SEMINARY LIBRARY
DARLINGTON, N. J. 07446

ology, "systematic" and "speculative," makes its appearance. It is a moral theology, however, that is quite different from the "speculative" moral theology of St. Thomas and St. Bonaventure. Two causes can be assigned for this: the reaction against the "Philosophy of the Enlightenment" (*Aufklärung*) and the development of the idealist philosophy. That "rational" Christianity, friend of the "enlightenment," which seemed to satisfy the preceding generation, is no longer wanted. Instead of the cold classical "Reason," the Romantics prefer sentiment, passion, impulse, and later on the will, even the unconscious.

On the other hand, when there is mention of "Idea" we should not imagine that we have to do with a simple principle of *exposition*, with a new way, more elegant and more attractive, of presenting Christian moral teaching. It must be understood that the "Idea" is *the reality itself* and that this reality is nothing more than the "development" of the Idea. Instead of a construction that might be termed "vertical," which considers man in himself, abstracted from time and subject to unchanging and eternal ethical laws, one would substitute a "horizontal" construction dominated by the notion of *development*. "Vitalism" makes its entry into theology, and the scope of moral theology will be to observe and analyse in history the progressive steps in the manifestation of the Spirit.

DARLINGTON SEMINARY LIBRARY
DARLINGTON, N. J. 07843

Something of this new approach is already to be found in the *Manual of Christian Moral Teaching* of J. M. SAILER (1751-1832). Witnessing a preoccupation already quite modern, this work is not destined for the clergy alone, but also for the educated laity,[6] Sailer, in fact, wished to write neither a purely philosophical moral teaching, not a moral theology in the strict sense of the term, but rather an Ethics which will be *simultaneously* a *Moral Teaching based on Reason* and *Christian Ethic*.[7] In attacking strongly the "Philosophy of the Enlightenment" (*Aufklärung*), Sailer maintains that Ethics is nothing without God, without Christ and without love. It must, of course, be conceded that philosophy can conceive of God as the supreme Truth, as the final end of human life, but it cannot furnish us with a complete moral teaching because it knows nothing about the state in which man originally came from the hands of God, about the fall and Redemption.[8] The moral teaching of the philosophers is certainly in a position to proclaim fortrightly the notions of law and conscience and it can prescribe that men should lead their lives "in conformity with reason." But what is the true origin of law and conscience? There is only one possible answer to this ques-

---

6. M. SAILER, *Handbuch der christlichen Moral zunächst für künftige Seelensorger und dann für jeden gebildeten Christen*, Munich 1817.

7. *Ibid.*, t. I, p. 110.

8. *Ibid.*, p. 14.

tion: God is at one and the same time the first cause both of free will and of law.[9] It does not matter much how we arrive at this fundamental assertion, whether by way of science or by that of "faith."[10] One thing is certain and that is, that God is the cause of all morality and the development of divine life in us in the goal of human life. Without wishing to deny the formula of the philosophers: act in conformity with "reason," Sailer quite evidently prefers another that sounds very modern indeed: work for the realization of the Eternal in time.[11]

The fundamental act of the moral life is the understanding of the relation that exists between the Law and God, an activity which Sailer calls "Religiosity."[12] But how is the transit made from this romantic "Religiosity" to the positive *Religion* of the Christian revelation? In other words, how is the transit made from this "religious" moral teaching to the revealed Ethics of the Gospel? Sailer gives no clear explanation to that.[13]

---

9. *Ibid.*, p. 34.

10. To be exact, it is not a question here of theological faith, but of faith in the sense of Jacobi, as has been shown by DR. G. FISCHER, *J. M. Sailer und F. H. Jacobi. Der Einfluss evangelischer Christen auf Sailers Erkenntnistheorie und Religionsphilosophie,* Fribourg-B. 1955.

11. SAILER, Handbuch, t. I, p. 46.

12. *Ibid.*, p. 48.

13. We should not forget that, for Sailer, there is only one Ethics which is found at different times in the intuitions of the Philosophers, in the voice of conscience and in the realities of the Christian life (cf. t. I, p. 122). To obey the voice of Christ is to obey conscience, since both have the same content (*ibid.* p. 195). The 32 propositions of the *Moral der Vernunft* con-

We must distinguish carefully between the moral teaching propounded by Christ and the Apostles, that moral teaching which has been lived and put into practice by Christians down the centuries, and the moral teaching of the "schools," or "moral theology." They are two quite different things. In moral theology the Christian moral message or teaching has become the object of speculation and has always been deeply influenced by the philosophy prevalent during the different periods of its history: thus we have the Platonism of the Fathers, the Aristotelianism of the scholastics, Cartesianism, idealist philosophy and so on. It does not seem that the Christian moral teaching has benefited by this treatment either in clarity or in force. In this unhappy mixture of the divine and human both suffer and in the end one finds there neither Christ nor Aristotle. It is, then, high time to return to a moral teaching that is thoroughly Christian.[14]

It is, however, J. B. HIRSCHER (1788-1865), the noted moralist of the Tubingen school, who more than anyone else merits our attention. According to Hirscher the moral life of the Christian is nothing else than the

---

stantly tell us about faith, the Eternal, Revelation, etc. All that can be said is that the distinction between the *etica naturalis* and *revealed* morality or moral teaching is not at all clear in the mind of the author, who wrote, it must be remember, more than half a century before the first Vatican Council.

14. *Handbuch*, I, p. 85.

revealed Truth itself in so far as it is active in man.[15]
Now, all the truths which Christ taught, all the institu-
tions which He founded (the Church, the sacraments)
may be reduced to the "idea" of the Kingdom of God.[16]
The "Kingdom of God" is at one and the same time the
center of all revealed Truth and the essence of the evolu-
tive process which, in the course of history, comes to
perfection little by little in souls. Consequently moral
theology will be nothing else than the science of the
progressive realization of the Kingdom of God in man,
whereas dogmatic theology will describe the progressive
evolution of dogmas, of the *objective* contents of the
Revelation of the Kingdom of God.[17].

For this reason it is a mistake to consider moral theology as a practical science.[18] On the contrary, it is part
of "systematic" theology. In fact there is only *one* theology whose business it is to study the Kingdom of God
in its double development, objective and subjective, in
the objective evolution of dogmas and in the concrete
realizations of the Christian life.

On the other hand, the Christian life is "organic,"
that is to say, it is completely informed by a *vital* princi-

---

15. J. B. HIRSCHER, *Die christliche Moral als Lehre von der Verwick-
lichung des göttlichen Reiches in der Menschheit*, Tübingen 1835, t. I, p. IV.
16. *Ibid.*
17. *Ibid.*, p. 3.
18. *Ibid.*

ple: the Spirit.[19] Moral theology will, as a consequence, have to guard against "rubricism"; it must not be satisfied with drawing up a list of duties and precepts. It is failed to take account of the vital principle of the Christian life, it would deem its work done when it elaborated moral structures that are lifeless and artificial. The moralists do doubtlessly attempt to superimpose on their sciences a "principle" to be the basis of its unity. But this principle remains for the most part extraneous to the Christian life, of which moral theology should paint for us a faithful image. Besides, the only authentic intuition of the Christian's moral duties cannot be attained until one has attained to the Living Principle which penetrates all the faculties of man and consecrates in a certain sense all the relations which he can entertain with others.[20]

It is also a mistake to begin the elaboration of moral theology with a consideration of *man* and an examination of his possibilities of action. The theologians, who have elaborated a moral theology, having once established this purely philosophical anthropology, attempt to pass on to a higher order of truths, that is, to the supernatural life. In reality, moral theology should proceed the other way about. It should start with the vital notion of the King-

19. *Ibid.*, p. 6.
20. *Ibid.*, p. VI.

dom of God and only then should it treat of the moral situation, of the possibilities which render man capable of entering the Kingdom of God.[21] The general plan of moral theology will consequently be set up in the following way: first and foremost it must treat of the Kingdom of God in itself; and afterwards of its progessive realization in man.

Moral theology, as worked out by Hirscher, will of necessity bear the mark of this essentially historical and genetical preoccupation. Already in the introduction he describes at length the history of the Christian life from apostolic times down to his own day.[22] In and since the Middle Ages this history is seen to be frequently a *conflict* between a "mosaico-Christian" conception or attitude, which develops above all a moral teaching based on prohibitions, and the authentically Christian (*rein christliche*) approach, according to which Christianity is first of all *interiority and freedom*.[23] The Christian moral teaching found itself first of all opposed to pagan customs, and then found that it had to fight against the crude habits of the barbarians. Before the Peace of Constantine it is dominated by the ideal of martyrdom, which is replaced later by the monastic ideal. Now, in moral theology the real business is to get beyond all

---

21. *Ibid.*, p. V.
22. *Ibid.*, pp. 38-80.
23. *Ibid.*, p. 58.

that and expound authentically, *in itself and for its own sake*, the Christian moral teaching. And here too the method of treatment will have to be dynamic and genetic. Hirscher, treating right at the start (Bk. I) of the Kingdom of God, begins with the divine plan of creation, leads through the account of the creation and the fall, on to the Redemption and the institution of the Church. When he goes on then (Bk. II) to consider the Kingdom of God in man, Hirscher commences with the birth and baptism of man and goes on to show his development up to the hour of death, pointing out exactly in what way, how he is subject, in the different periods of his life, to both the sacramental and teaching activity of the Church. It is at the beginning of this second book (part 1) that Hirscher introduces the study of "the possibilities of man in the ethical order": man is person, freedom, conscience, but also affectivity through which he becomes the "subject" of love.

All this still tells us nothing about the "imitation" of Christ (*Nachfolge Christi*) nor does it tell us anything about the personal relationship that should unite every Christian to Christ. We have to wait for the Manual (*Lehrbuch*) of KONRAD MARTIN (1812-1879) to find this principle of imitation formulated. According to Martin, who later became Bishop of Paderborn, moral theology is the science which teaches us to direct our actions according to the doctrine and example of Christ. The axiom:

always act as a true imitator or follower of Christ (als ächste Nachfolger Christi) becomes the supreme "principle" of the Christian moral teaching.[24]

On the other hand a moral teaching that wishes to be authentically Christian cannot remain enclosed within the limits of the "pagan" or "Greek" or "scholastic" scheme of the four cardinal virtues. Before and above these, for example, one will place the virtue of humility. Such an attack upon the "Greek" virtues, quite mode today, is to be found already in the work of M. JOCHAM (1808-1893).

Finally, the desire to construct "a moral teaching of the Mystical Body" will bring with it as a result the *transposition* of sacramental morality. In the classical plan of the manuals this sacramental morality came in third place after fundamental moral theology and "the ethics of duties or obligations" (the precepts), unless one prefer to follow the order of the "virtues." In the work of Jocham, on the contrary, sacramental moral theology comes before the *Pflichtenlehre*, the ethics of obligations, which itself is entirely centered around the theological virtues, faith, hope and charity. When expounding sacramental moral theology Jocham places Orders and Matrimony before the Eucharist, because their "communitary" character is more apparent.[25] The early

---

24. Cf. HADROSSEK, *op. cit.*, p. 107.
25. *Ibid.*, pp. 198-203.

Christians would certainly have been very surprised had they been told that the Eucharist is not the "communitary" act par excellence.

These investigations, however cursory, enable us to evaluate what is really new in the famous "new tendencies" in moral theology. What is truly new is this and this alone: the references, whether explicit or not, to the philosophy of Scheler, that is the "principle of personal exemplarity" and the concept of "engagement" or personal involvement according to the example of the person-model (*Vorbild*). Perhaps this philosophy is already out-moded. It is for all that necessary to expound its essential traits with reference to the point that interests us, if we wish to understand exactly, from a philosophical point of view, the significance of the "new" moral theology.[26]

* * *

According to Scheler the higher values are personal values. Consequently, the person who is the bearer or subject of the highest values will be, for other persons, the exemplar or model of all behavior, of the whole of

---

26. The most recent work on Scheler is: M. DUPUY, *La philosophie de Max Scheler*, Paris 1959. See also by the same author: *La philosophie de la religion chez Max Scheler*, Paris 1959.

moral existence.[27] For Kant the essence of morality consists in obedience to the Law; a concrete and personal model cannot enter into account except to prove the *non-impossibility* of fulfilling the precept. It is completely different for Scheler. *Before* exercising any action in conformity with norms and *before* any kind of education the moral person must be "taken in charge" by another person or by the idea which he forms of this person.[28] "Respect" for the norm presupposes respect for the "Person-model" and even more the *love* which one has for it.

The basis for this position is clearly explained in the short work *Models and Leaders*.[29] In every person there exists a radical orientation to love or to hate.[30] The "possibility" and the determination of the person's existence in the world are both radically conditioned by this.[31] The person is raised in that way above the *esse mundanum,* which is essentially finite and is at the origin of the mechanistic science and conception of the universe.

---

27. M. SCHELER, *Der Formalismus in der Ethik und die materiale Wertethik,* ed. 3, Halle 1927, p. 282. It should be noted that for Scheler the "Person-model" is an "individual axiological essence." To make of it a moral norm and to declare it to be the supreme norm, is to miss his thought altogether. The norm is, by definition, universal and impersonal.

28. *Ibid.,* p. 599.

29. Cf. Chap. 1, note 2.

30. The translation of *Grundgesinnung* by "état d'esprit" (Gandillac, Dupuy)—state of mind—weakens considerably the importance of this word. One has to do here with a fundamental intuition of the person, with a grasping of the "meaning" of the person.

31. *Vorbilder und Führer,* p. 264.

For Scheler the "person of value" is, as indeed are all values, something *objective*. It is not merely a construction of the subjectivity. But it is not by reasoning, by reflection, nor by "sentiment" that "the fundamental orientation of one's mentality," of which we have spoken, is in any way actuated. The person of value is comprehended, by the one who imitates it, in an "emotional intuition" (the heart has reasons which the reason itself does not know). This emotional intuition is for all practical purposes identifiable with love. And we know already that, over against the person-model, there is to be found its opposed counter-part: "anti-models," which are an object of avoidance and repulsion. In this case hate takes the place of love. Thus we arrive at the fundamental proposition: *"before* singular individual actions are either accepted or repelled by the moral mentality, *before* values are recognized as such or rejected, *before* obedience is given to commands or there be refusal to obey, there is the affirmation of love or the rejection of hate towards a *person* considered in its totality as a person of value."[32]

We know how equivocal the term "personalism" is. According to the old belief, wrote ELLEN KEY, true personality, in the most profound depths of human existence, consisted in the realization of those superior values

---

32. *Ibid.*, p. 272.

that are ultimately *common* to the individual and to others. For the new belief, on the contrary, personality is that which is absolutely individual, that which the person does not have in common with any other.[33] From that derive important consequences on the ethical level. "Nature" will correspond to that which is vulgar or coarse, to the anonymous (to the "one,"); "person" will correspond to that which is "noble," to the absolutely personal values, to the "I" as opposed to the "mass." Will there be any need, then, to emphasize the superiority of the person over the common or vulgar norms? Logically one will be forced to admit that the "cessation" of the common or vulgar moral teaching, of the morality of norms and precepts, be a possibility in the name of the absolute axiological *superiority* of the person. It is in that precise way that the religious philosophy of Kierkegaard understood the faith of Abraham as manifested in the sacrificing of Isaac. Here faith would imply a real suspending of moral obligation or precept.[34] It does

---

33. Quoted by TILLMAN, *Die Idee der Nachfolge* p. 60. Tillmann points out quite correctly that the ancient theologians did not neglect completely that which is absolutely personal, and that the idolatry of the Ego understood in this way is rather a caricature of true personalism.

34. In the case of the sacrifice of Isaac (the putting to death of an innocent person) the ancient theologians saw a *dispensation* in the precepts of the second table of the legislation of Sinai, a dispensation which God alone has the right to accord. St. Thomas, who at one time admitted this explanation, adopts later on a different one (cf. I-II, q. 94, a. 5, ad 2). Were one to admit that a person could *dispense himself* in the name of an absolutely "individual value," that would be the very essence of "situation" Ethics.

not at all seem that anything of the kind is to be found in Scheler and consequently he cannot be considered as one of the fathers of situation ethics. Against the universalism of Kant he extolled, on the contrary, the personal values, those, namely, that give rise to a type of obligation that is valid for one person only. As a consequence, each person must cultivate in a special way the axiological qualities that are proper to it. But Scheler adds: *"without forgetting,* however, the values that he has in common with others."[35] Besides, every person must contribute to the whole of the community formed by the persons. Thus, for Scheler, solidarity does away with individualism.[36]

The whole moral system of Scheler, however, cannot be understood except in connection with his negative position in the question of the *precept* of love. Scheler maintains, as Kant did, that it is contradictory and impossible to constitute love the object of a precept.[37] The precept of faith itself means quite simply that we are bound to put ourselves into the situation of having the faith, as, for instance, by acquiring a sufficient knowledge of the truths to be believed. As far as it is concerned, the precept of charity aims at nothing more than external *beneficence,* which is an effect of charity, and not at its

35. SCHELER, *Der Formalismus* . . . , p. 512.
36. Cf. DUPUY, *La philosophie de Max Scheler,* pp. 551-55.
37. SCHELER, *Der Formalismus* . . . , p. 224-225.

internal *act*. In fact, if it be true that this act consist in the *spontaneity* and *freedom*, which it implies, then the precept is useless. On the contrary, if the act be placed, *quia praeceptum*, the interior intention, which the law purports to demand, that, namely of a free and spontaneous activity, will be found to be frustrated.[38] Finally, the great precept of love is seen to be reduced to an "invitation" to *follow* Christ.[39] Of course, the

---

38. In this connection it is well to recall the remarks of S. Kierkegaard. According to K., no matter how joyous and ineffable be love, it always feels the need of *binding itself*. When love has become duty, only then is it eternally assured. This security and steadfastness, which eternity gives, does away with all unease and makes love perfect. For the first spontaneous love that is satisfied with just existing, is inseparable from a certain *anguish*, that namely of being able *to change*. True love, on the contrary, that has taken on the character of eternity by becoming *duty*, never changes. And Kierke-gaard concludes: only when love has become duty is it eternally free, in a felicitous dependence (*Vie et règne de l'amour*, trad. Villadsen, Paris, s. d., pp. 39-49). Here Kierkegaard is thinking of conjugal love, but the very same principles can be applied to the love of God and here, we discover again the echo of the "freedom" of St. Augustine. We should also mention that St. Thomas, in connection with charity (II-II, q. 44, a 1 ad 2), proposes and discusses a difficulty very close to that of Kant and Scheler.

39. The "material Ethic of values" is not simply a refutation of the "formalism" of Kant and of Eudemonism (known and the rejected by Kant) but is also the rejection of every Ethic of finality and of "reason." Scheler does, without doubt, give a large place to finality (*Ziel*) as imminent in the tendencies of the human being. But, with Kant, he rejects every Ethic of "ends, or goals or purposes" (*Zweck*), perceived by reason or the imagina-tion, because such a moral teaching leads inevitably to empiricism, to which is opposed the apriorism of Kant. Scheler also discards every "Ethic of human nature," that is, every moral teaching which seek in the *ontological* structure of man the foundation of the moral norm. Reason is something simple. Nor does man, according to Scheler, correspond to one single biolog-ical species. He is the purely contingent product of various lines of parallel evolution (Formalismus . . . , pp. 279-280). Still less can there be question of admitting the notion of an unchangeable human "essence" in the sense of

theologians who have drawn inspiration from the ideas of Scheler, have very wisely left this point in the background, although it is essential to his thought.

* * *

Let us return to the "principle of exemplarity." It does not mean exclusively the necessity of integrating concrete *examples* into every moral teaching: *exempla trahunt*, affirms repeatedly the wisdom of the ages. The real point at issue is this: the comprehension of values and norms presupposes in the moral agent a prior adhering to the "Person-Model," an adhering which is rooted in love.

Now, such a doctrine comes up against grave objections.[40] The decisive act by which the subject commits itself to "following in the footsteps" of the *Vorbild*, of the "person-model," cannot exist without a *judgment*, that is, without the judgment by which one discerns in the other the "person of value," that will become from then on the exemplar of morality. Otherwise why choose one "person as exemplar" rather than another? Why

---

classical ontology. The result is that the values must be something either inferior or superior to man. They cannot be something specifically human (*Formalismus . . .* , p. 283). Scheler, whilst severely criticizing Nietzsche, agrees with him for all that in maintaining that man must be "surpassed."

40. These criticisms were formulated by N. HARTMANN, *Ethik*, ed, 3, Berlin 1949, pp. 129-131.

Jesus instead of Zarathustra, Socrates or Zeno? Why too reject the negative models, the "anti-models"? If all this is not to be founded on a blind choice, then it must necessarily be admitted that the subject, before "following" as a "disciple" such or such a person of value, has precisely recognized in that person the presence of values, of certain axiological qualities. But such a judgment is possible only if the moral subject is *already in possession* of its own "scale" of values. It is consequently not true to say that the decisive act of adhering to the model or exemplar *precedes* the *comprehension* of values. Quite the opposite is true. Were it otherwise, the values would not be known *a priori* in an act of pure intuition, but would be the result of a purely empirical and fortuitous adhering to such or such another "person of value."

Scheler himself admitted that no historical personality, however great, exhausts completely one or more of the types of "persons of value" analysed by him: the saint, the genius, the hero. But how, then, is one to judge of the presence or absence of values in any particular saint, in any particular genius or in any particular hero, if the criterion according to which may be judged in what measure the subject will be able to place himself under their guidance, to allow himself to be "taken in charge" by them, be not first of all established? The act of personal commitment to the following of the "person-model" should never in any case be reduced to a purely irrational impulse of sacred enthusiasm. Such an act would have nothing to do with that freedom which, according to Scheler, as indeed for every form of personalism, is the inalienable privilege of the "person." On the other hand it may be asked: is the *Nachfolge*, the "imitation," to be a kind of blind faith? Is no doubt, no critical reflection whatever to be admitted concerning the dogma of the perfection of the model and its infallibility? Scheler himself teaches the contrary. And that implies subordinating the act which decides the "imitation" or following to the foregoing knowledge or judgment concerning the values present.

There would, however, be one solution to all this: and that would be to see in God himself the "person of value" who is to constitute for us the principle by which we come to a knowledge of the values and is at the same time the perfect exemplar of their concrete realization. Besides, God is indefectible perfection itself. We will consequently have the assurance of not being obliged to subject the person to the values, but rather shall we in a position to show without the slightest difficulty that the values *have their origin* in the "person-model." But Scheler rejected this solution. God cannot constitute *for us* the "person of value" *par excellence*, the supreme *Vorbild* of human morality, and that precisely on account of His infinitude itself. In a certain sense it is contradictory that a finite person should take as personal exemplar of his acts an infinite person.[41]

On the level of a purely "natural" morality, in a state of "pure nature" it would have to be admitted that the objections of Scheler in this matter are very well founded. In fact, the more or less inexact or confused knowledge of a personal God and that immediate and intimate interpersonal relation which the personal act of "involvement" placing the subject under the dominion of the "person-model" implies are two quite different things. Such a gift of self demands an answer on the part of the "person-model." The moral teaching of the "imitation," the morality of the "imitation" implies a *dialogue*, not a kind of monologue of despair. And that means that the total involvement, the *Nachfolge*, implies already a friendship between the persons concerned. But is friendship possible between man and God in the purely natural order? We would seem to be justified in denying it.[42] And if friendship is impossible, must we not also cease maintaining that all morality, even purely natural morality, has as its foundation a radical interpersonal relationship binding the moral subject to God as exemplar and the immediate model of all moral activity?

The Christian life, on the contrary, seems to be in a position to do full justice to the moral teaching of

---

41. SCHELER, *Der Formalismus* . . . , p. 612.
42. St. Thomas, III Sent., dist. 27, q. a. 2 ad 4.

personal exemplarity. For the Christian, Christ is something much more than the "hero," the "genius" and the "saint" as analysed by Scheler in his description of "persons of value." Because he is God, Christ can be and in fact *is* the source of all value, he can make a claim to that absolute confidence, that total submission which the human heroes, and men of genius and saints cannot demand with the same right and in the same degree. From Christ we derive all religious values and from his grace we receive the power to incarnate them, in a certain sense, in our lives. We have thus arrived back at the point of departure. After this long exposition let us now attempt to examine the matter in itself in the light of the "principles" of St. Thomas' teaching.

III What Does "Imitation" Mean?

The Latin word *imitari*, from which are derived all the terms used in Romance languages is a frequentative verbal form related to the word *imago*, and it means, in the strict sense of the term, to strive to reproduce the image. In this sense imitation is as old as man himself and the philosophers, ever since men began to philosophize, have never neglected devoting attention to it. According to the ancient Democritus, men learned the practice of the arts by observing and imitating the animals: by observing the spiders man learned how to weave and sew.[1] According to Aristotle, it is second nature to man from his infancy to imitate.[2] It is with Plato that the philosophy of imitation takes on a very special importance. For Plato, time imitates Eternity,[3] the visible world, being a participation of the world of ideas, is also an imitation of it.[4] We thus arrive at the "cosmo-

---

1. HERMANN DIELS, *Die Fragmente der Vorsokratiker*, Griechisch und Deutsch, 3 Bde, herausgegeben von Walter Kranz, Weidmannsche Verlagsbuchhandlung, Berlin 5 1934 ff. Democritus of Abdera, Fragment n° 154.

2. ARISTOTLE, *Poet.*, 4, 1448 b 5.

3. PLATO, *Tim.*, 38 a.

4. *Ibid.*, 48 e.

logical," *metaphysical*, concept of imitation: one thing can be in so far as it is the imitation of another. Thus it is that Virgil will compare the buzzing of the bees to the sound of the trumpet:

> .... a voice
> *Like* (*imitata*) trumpets' hollow sounds is heard.
> (Georg. IV, 71-72)

But akin to this "physical" meaning of imitation (one thing which *is* in imitation of another), the concept of imitation understood in a *moral* sense quickly makes its appearance: no longer *to be* but *to act* in imitation of another. Here again we find the program or ideal of Plato: we must fly and escape from the things of here below in order to become like to God.[5] The Stoics take up the same idea: to honor the gods, says Seneca, means to imitate them.[6] Alongside this authentic and true imitation there is also the false and spurious, that, namely, of the evil man who takes on the *appearances* of the good man. It is in that way that an evil political regime takes on the appearances of a good one.[7]

The Platonic notion of the cosmological imitation of the Ideas, platonic exemplarism, is not to be found in the Bible. The rabbinic writers did, however, already

---

5. PLATO, *Theet.*, 176 b; *Laws* IV, 716 c-d; *Phaedro*, 253 b.
6. SENECA, *Letter* 95.
7. PLATO, *Pol.* 293.

point out that man, as image of God, should as a consequence imitate God.[8]

While the words *miméomai, mimēma* are found very rarely in the Septuagint version of the Bible, the Old Testament, on its part, very frequently brings forward an idea that is quite close to it, the idea, namely, of *walking with God*. This semitic expression is, without any doubt, of cultual origin.[9] It signifies first and foremost the liturgical *procession*, in which the people follow or *walk* behind the image of the divinity, an image that is normally shut up in the obscure depths of the temples. It is in this sense that the people of Israel quite materially follow Jahweh across the desert, for He goes before the people in a cloud or in a pillar of fire (*Ex*. 13, 21).

But it is in the moral and no longer in the physical sense that the following is said: *Enoch ... walked with God* (*Gen*. 5, 24). The same is said of Noah (*Gen*. 6, 9), of Abraham (17, 1) and of Jacob (48, 15). To walk after Jahweh is to observe his commandments (*Ex*. 16, 4; *Lev*. 26, 3; *Deut*. 5, 33; 11, 22; *II Kings* 23, 3). But this observance of the commandments is not always reduced to a cold "legalism." A proof of that is the magnificent eulogy of David, which the prophet Abias addressed to the queen, the wife of Jeroboam: ... *my servant David*

---

8. Cf. J. BONSIRVEN, *Le Judaisme palestinien au temps de Jésus-Christ,* Paris 1935, t. II, p. 42.

9. Cf. G. KITTEL, *Theol. Wörterbuch z. NT.*, t. V.

. . . *who observed my precepts and followed me with
all his heart, doing only that which is pleasing to me*
(*J Kings* 14, 8).

In the New Testament "to follow" also has at times
the material sense of walking after: the crowds follow
Jesus (Mark 3, 7). But in Matthew 19, 21: COME,
FOLLOW ME, is an invitation to become a disciple, to
follow Jesus by adopting his manner of life, his way of
suffering, of poverty, of the Cross (*Matt.* 8, 20; *Mark* 8,
34), of humility (*John* 13, 15) and above all of charity
(*John* 13, 34). Have we not thus arrived at the notion
of the imitation of Christ? *For what does "to follow"
mean if not "to imitate"* (St. Augustine, *De s. virg.*, 27,
PL 40, 411).

In the writings of St. Paul (and also in III John 11)
we come up against a frequent use of the terms *miméomai*
(4 times), *mimētēs* (7 times): *Be imitators of me as J
am of Christ* (*J Cor.* 11, 1; cf. 4, 16); *Be then imitators
of God, as becomes dearly beloved sons* (*Eph.* 5, 1).[10]

---

10. It does not pertain to our plan, nor indeed is it of our competence, to
expound the questions, discussed in modern exegesis, concerning these famous
texts of St. Paul. We can, however, get some idea of the matter by consulting
B. RIGAUX, O.F.M., *Les Epîtres aux Thessaloniciens*, Paris, 1956, pp. 380-
382; D. M. Stanley, S.J. in Bibl. 40 (1959) 859-877. A good number of
Protestant exegetes hesitate a great deal with regard to the imitation understood in the "ethical" sense, they mistrust the idea of the imitation of Christ's
virtues, of his "style" of life. This is easily understandable. To admit the
imitatio Christi, is to admit the value of "works," and offend against the
Protestant dogma of *iustificatio sola fide*: it is to open the door to the doctrine

of merit: *Sequi Salvatorem participare est salutem,* wrote St. Irenaeus (*Haer.,* V, 14, 1, PG 7, 1010; Harvey, t. II, p. 184).

With regard to ancient or primitive Christianity it is a great exaggeration to say that "if there was a great love for Christ to be found in the primitive Christians, they saw in him less the Man than God, the eternal Son of the Father,... their love seems to have been more strong than tender" (A. SAUDRAU, *La piété à travers les âges,* Angers 1927, p. 231). Such a sweeping statement must needs be totally ignored. Cf. POURRAT, *La spiritualité chrétienne,* t. I, p. 368; VILLER-RAHNER, *Asxese und Mystik in der Väterzeit,* 294-302; A. HEITMANN, *Imitatio Dei. Die ethische Nachahmung Gottes nach der Väterlehre der zwei ersten Jahrhunderte,* Rome 1940; I. HAUSHERR, *L'imitation de Jésus-Christ dans la spiritualité byzantine,* Mélanges Cavallera, Toulouse 1948, pp. 231-259.

IV   The Imitation of Christ
in the Teaching of St. Thomas

In his big systematic works St. Thomas makes but few references to the theme of the imitation of Christ, but these few are beautiful indeed and profound. "The Christian," he says, "is he who belongs to Christ. To belong to Christ is not just to have faith in Christ, it also means to practice the virtues in the spirit of Christ and to die to sin in imitation of Christ, as is said in the Epistle to the Galatians (5, 24): *Those who belong to Christ Jesus have crucified the flesh with its passions and desires*."[1] In another place St. Thomas insists that the perfection of the religious life consists above all in the imitation of Christ.[2]

In writing his commentaries on the works of St. Paul he came upon the words: *be imitators of me as I am of Christ*.[3] He was able, as a result, to offer us a broader synthesis on this subject and here we can clearly detect

---

1. St. Thomas, II-II, q. 124, a. 5 ad 1.

2. *Ibid.*, q. 186, a. 5, sed contra.

3. In *I Cor.* 11, 1. This, as is known, is a "reportatum" made by the students, not the text composed by St. Thomas himself. That which immediately precedes is taken from the Postilla *Dedi te* of Peter of Tarantaise (Innocent V). See also: *I Cor.* 4, 16; *Eph.* 5, 1; *Phil.* 3 ,17; *I Thess.* 1, 6; *II Thess.* 3, 7-9; *Hebr.* 6, 12; 13, 7.

the influence of Denis. The essential elements of his synthesis can be set down as follows. It is in the order of things that the lower beings should imitate, as far as they can, those beings that are superior to them. The first exemplar in the order of being and in their coming into existence is nothing else than the Son of God. Consequently all creatures imitate him as the true and perfect image of the Father. In a special way the Word is the exemplar of the gifts of grace found in spiritual creatures. But this exemplar was at first very distant from us: "who is man, to be able to walk in the footsteps of his king?" The Son of God consequently wished to become man as well in order to offer to men the model of a human life. It remains now to be explained how Paul could offer himself as exemplar of life and living to the Christians of Corinth. Referring explicitly to Denis,[4] St. Thomas points out that the eternal Exemplar is imitated, first and foremost, by the higher spirits in the hierarchy of being, and then by the other and lower beings. In the same way, the living example of the life of Christ is proposed first and foremost for the imitation of the prelates, who are to become in their turn true models of

---

4. PSEUDO-DENIS, *De Cael. Hier.*, c. 4, translation of John Scotus Eriugena (Dionysiaca, II, 803-805): sanctae caelestium essentiarum dispositiones super ea quae tantum *sunt et* irrationabilia *viventia,* secundumque nos *rationalia,* in hierarchiae participatione factae sunt. Indivisibiliter enim in divinam imitationem seipsas reformantes ... copiosiores ad eam habent communiones.

life for their flocks, but only in the measure in which they themselves are imitators of Christ.[5]

We should not, however, imagine that the prelates, superiors and saints in any way conceal Christ, that they interpose themselves like an opaque screen between the faithful and Christ. Seeing that they are his living image, they refer back to the supreme model, to the exemplar of which they are but imperfect imitations. The Christian imitates Christ in the very process of imitating the saints. Thomistic metaphysics has something akin to this to offer us. The action of the second causes does not do away with that of the first cause, which belongs to an absolutely transcendent order. The doctrine of Denis concerning hierarchical mediation, as understood by St. Thomas, does not preclude God being, directly and immediately, the principle and the *causa conversiva* of each and everything that is.[6]

IMITATION IN THE PHILOSOPHY OF ST. THOMAS

The doctrine of imitation occupies a big place in thomist thought. St. Thomas never tires of repeating that

5. II-II, q. 43, a. 5.

6. St. Thomas thinks that Denis wishes to refute the "Platonici" on this point (cf. In Dion., *De div. Nom.*, c. 1, lect. 3, ed. Pera n. 100). In Proclus, being, life, intelligence are brought back to three distinct principles: the First Being, the First Life and the First Intelligence. Cf. PROCLUS, *Elem. Theologica*, translation of William of Moerbeke, Prop. 101, ed. C. Vansteenkiste, TiF 1951, 490. On Denis' thought concerning this matter, cf. R. REQUES, *L'univers dionysien*, Paris 1954, pp. 80-81.

all creatures are "imitations" of divine Ideas. Essence, existence, being and acting, everything proceeds from the divine ideas and is the imitation of them.[7] Since God made everything in the supreme decree of his Wisdom, nothing ever happens without His having willed it or foreseen it. When the creature fulfills that which God willed for it, it imitates "the will" of God.[8]

Taken in this very broad sense, the idea of imitation comes very close to that of *participation*. Where there is participation, there also is imitation.[9] But the two concepts do not coincide completely: for participation implies, between that which is participated and that which participates, an ontological distance, an inferiority (*partem capere, to contain a part*), which imitation does not always entail. There can be perfect *equality* between him who imitates and him who is imitated. For that reason it is not to the notion of participation, but rather to that of image that St. Thomas, in the last analysis, attaches, the notion of imitation: *it is of the very essence of an image to consist in imitation. . . . It is indeed called an image as if it were* IMITAGO.[10]

---

7. I, q. 9, a. 1 ad 2: nihil esse potest quod non procedat a divina Sapientia per quandam *imitationem.* Cf. I Sent. dist. 36, q. 2, a. 3.

8. II Sent. dist. 1, q. 1, a. 2 ad 3: unaquaeque res maxime ad suum finem accedit, quando imitatur divinam voluntatem, secundum quod de ipsa . . . dispositum est a Deo.

9. I Sent., dist. 48, q. 1, a. 1: quod participative habet formam, *imitatur* illud quod essentialiter habet.

10. I Sent., dist. 28, q. 2, a.

It is only the creature which is endowed with intelligence that is in the image of God. In the lower creatures we find no more than the vestiges or traces (of God), which give us only a very feeble idea of the divine perfections, just as the imprint of a step in the sand does not tell us at all who or what the man is who left it there in passing. And for all that the simple trace or vestige is already an imitation of the divine perfections.[11] But this is much more perfect in the *image*, which represents God *in specie naturae*,[12] because in the image we find intelligence, will and memory. But the image also implies degrees. In man and in the angel, in spite of their greatness, the image remains very imperfect. The Son of God alone is the perfect *image* of the Father,[13] whereas

11. I Sent. 3, 2, 2: vestigium invenitur in creatura in quantum *imitatur* divinam perfectionem.

12. II Sent., dist. 16, q. 1, a. 2: intellectualis natura attingit ad *imitationem* divinam, in qua quodammodo consistit species naturae eius; et inde est quod in eadem operatione ponimus ultimam felicitatem intellectualis creaturae, in qua est felicitas Dei, scilicet in contemplatione intellectiva.

It seems that this text should be corrected as follows: *in quo* (not: *in qua*) *quodammodo consistit species naturae ipsius,* according to MSS. Vat. lat. 5. 716 and Chigi B, V, 17.

13. I Sent., dist. 28, q. 2, a. 1 ad 3: perfectissima ratio imaginis est quando eamdem numero formam et naturam invenimus in imitante cum eo quem imitatur et sic est Filius perfectissima imago Patris.—Cf. I, 93, 1.—St. Thomas at times opposes the "similitudo imitationis" to the "similitudo aequiparantiae," cf. II-II, 163, 2 (and also I, 63, 3; II Sent. dist. 22, q. 1, a. 2; *de Malo*, 16, 3 ad 15). Neither Adam nor the angels could have desired the "similitudo aequiparantiae." The same distinction is made with regard to conformity to the will of God: *voluntas hominis non potest conformari voluntati divinae per aequiparantiam, sed per imitationem* (I-II, 19, 9 ad 1). It is evident that, in all this, "imitation" is opposed to equality and is understood on the level of *participation*.

the angel and man are rather *ad imaginem Dei*, in the image of God, they are not the image of God.

We have already seen that Greek philosophy had learned to distinguish a double meaning of imitation: understood, namely, either in the "ontological" sense (one being which *is* in imitation of another . . .), or in the "ethical" sense (*to act* in imitation of . . .). This fundamental distinction was not unknown to St. Thomas. Only the free creature, capable of ordaining itself freely to an end, and of taking upon itself its own "responsibilities," is capable of *acting* in the true sense of the term. Only in that way is it capable of *choosing* a model of action, an exemplar that it wishes to follow, which indeed it wishes to follow *freely*, taking inspiration from the model, *adapting* its example to the circumstances, and not being a purely mechanical and servile copy. Consequently, only a creature endowed with intelligence is in a position *to will* to imitate an exemplar and to determine in its own way the modalities of its imitation.[14]

If understood, then, in its formal sense, in the "ethical" sense, imitation can pertain only to *persons*. The

---

14. *Ver.*, q. 3, a. 1: Si vero aliquid fiat *ad imitationem* alterius per agens quod *non derterminat sibi finem*, non ex hoc forma imitata rationem *exemplaris* vel ideae habet: non enim dicimus quod forma hominis generantis sit idea vel exemplar hominis generati, sed solum hoc dicimus quando agens . . . *determinat sibi finem.*—Cf. In *De Causis*, 14, ed. Saffrey, p. 86.

sole *subject* of action is the person. But what about the exemplar? Must it not also be a person? That being the case we will have arrived at the *principle* of personal exemplarity in the very context of scholastic philosophy itself using the methods proper to it, at the principle which may be formulated as follows: each and every one, in the context of his moral life, has a person-model, a *Vorbild*, whose traits and characteristics he strives to reproduce. We shall discuss this matter at length later (Chapter V).

One last remark. It is impossible to imitate a person without imitating him *in some precise matter*.[15] Imitation can have a limited object. One may imitate a gesture, a way of speaking, a manner of judging or of acting. One may also wish to imitate the whole, "to take all." But such a global imitation could not mean the absence of all determinations. To imitate all or the whole implies an enormous quantity of partial possibilities of which the person is the center of irradiation. A man has not just one sole action; he arrives at perfection and completion only through an almost infinite number of actions, of acts of will, of intentions and of affections. This will also hold good with reference to the imitation of Christ.

---

15. I Sent., dist. 28, q. 2, a. 1: de ratione imitationis duo consideranda sunt: *illud in quo* est imitatio et *illa quae* se se imitantur. Cf. II Sent., dist. 26, q. 1, a. 2 ad 5.

THE IMITATION OF CHRIST AND ST. THOMAS

Let us get back to St. Thomas's commentary on *1 Cor.*, ch. 11. When we read the phrase: *the Son of God is the exemplar or model which all creatures imitate in so far as he is the true and perfect image of the Father*, the preceding analysis leads us to understand these words as referring to imitation taken in the "ontological" sense, namely, to the imitation that is found in all creatures. On the contrary, the words: *the Word wished to become man so that he might present a human example to men. ... The example of his humanity is proposed for imitation first and foremost to the prelates of the Church*, constitute an appeal, an invitation to "dynamic" imitation, to that kind of imitation which supposes in him who imitates the free choice of the model. From the ontological order we have passed on to the sphere of ethics or moral life.

This chosen model is not the God of the philosophers according to the ideal envisaged by Plato.[16] The Christian is invited to imitate the Father of our Lord Jesus Christ: *Be then imitator of God, as beloved children*,[17] for it is only right and fitting that a son should imitate his Father and we are sons of God by adoption.[18] But,

---

16. Cf. Chap. 3, note 4.

17. *Eph.* 5, 1.

18. *St. Thomas*, In Epist. ad Ephes., lect. 1: imitandus est (Deus) taliter quomodo habemus possibilitatem, quia *ad filium pertinet patrem imitari.*

here below, the adoptive son does not see the Father; the inner life of the Trinity, of which he bears within himself the living image, remains hidden to him. How, then, "in imitation" of the divine exemplar, in imitation of the Father? The answer is, by imitating the Son of God become man in time. From now on it is possible to imitate God by imitating Christ. But, we may well ask, by imitating Christ in what way, in what precise things? Here too we have St. Paul's answer: *and walk in love, as Christ also loved us.*[19] Christ is imitated by the mutual exercise of love, by the forgiving of injuries, whereby we imitate at the same time the Father, who has pardoned us in Christ: *forgiving one another, as God also forgave you in Christ.*[20]

In St. John it is Christ who offers himself to us as the perfect example for the fulfillment of the precept: *that just as I loved you, you also love one another.*[21] St. Thomas lists certain elements in this exemplarism. The charity of Christ is the exemplar of ours by reason of its supreme and absolute "gratuity." For Christ first loved us without waiting for us to love him. It is for us to do the same: *we should then take the initiative in loving our neighbor, and not wait to be anticipated in our love, or make it dependent upon favors received.* Secondly, the

---

19. *Eph.* 5, 2. St. Thomas comments: ponit imitandi modum, quia in caritate.
20. *Eph.* 4, 31.
21. *John* 13, 34.

charity of Christ is the exemplar of ours by reason of its superhuman effectiveness. It was St. Gregory the Great who said: *The acid test of love is action and deed* (*in Ev.* Hom. 30, PL. 76, 1221). Now, Christ has shown us his love by his death, reminding us that there can be no greater proof of love than that which consists in dying for one's friends. St. Thomas draws the conclusion that we, too, should love one another not only in word, but also *in deed and in truth*. Finally, the charity of Christ was a love of perfect moral rectitude: *he loved us . . . disinterestedly*. This last remark refers to the foundation of love. St. Thomas, who takes for granted here his doctrine of charity as friendship, points out that friendship is *"recte"* (upright, straight-forward, selfless) when it is based on likeness or similitude, on "communication" (which is at the same time community and communion), in the true good. This kind of friendship is thus essentially opposed to utilitarian and hedonistic friendship, which seeks only its own pleasure. Taking for granted these distinctions, it is clear that the friendship-charity of Christ was in no way characterized by the traits of friendship-utility or hedonist friendship. It was, then, a completely selfless friendship founded on the divine similitude that comes from the grace of adoption.[22] And

---

22. ST. THOMAS, In Joann. c. 13, 34, lect. 7: *illa est recta amicitia quae est propter similitudinem seu communicationem in bono. Christus autem in tantum dilexit nos, inquantum similes sumus ei per gratiam adoptionis.*—We should not imagine, however, that Christ loves us *because* we are like him

here is the "pastoral" application of all this which St. Thomas proposes to us: *let* us love in our neighbor that which is of or belongs to God, *quod Dei est,* and not the benefits which we receive from him nor the pleasure he gives us.

*　　*　　*

There is to be found, then, in St. Thomas's commentaries on St. Paul and St. John a perfectly clear doctrine of "the imitation of Christ" in charity, a doctrine that is completely "biblical" in tone and character in spite of certain Dionysian[23] influence or "interferences." That being the case, why is it, then, that in his vast moral

---

through the grace of adoption. In reality, it is because he loves us that he makes us like unto himself. Otherwise the love of Christ would no longer be absolutely "gratuitous." But does not this gratuity consist precisely in dying for one's enemies rather than for one's friends, and is it not a greater "proof" of love to die for one's enemies than for one's friends? In his commentary on *John* 15, 13 St. Thomas replies to this question: *ad quod dicendum, quod Christus non posuit animam suam pro nobis inimicis, ut scilicet inimici remaneremus, sed ut amicos efficeret.* That is just a straight-forward application of the thomistic principles concerning charity towards one's enemies. In fact, charity does not consist in loving one's enemies, *as enemies,* or in taking pleasure in the fact that we are detested. That would be a sign of "will to power" much more than of evangelical gentleness. To love one's enemies means to love them *even though they be enemies,* in spite of the evil they do one. It means also desiring that they become friends. St. Thomas gives no other reply here in the case of Christ. It should be added that the text of II-II, 27, 7 which compares the love of enemies with the love of friends makes no mention of Christ.

23. It is one thing to use philosophy in explaining Sacred Scripture and quite another thing to become the slave of philosophy and subordinate the word of God to it: *cum enim gratia non tollit naturam ... oportet quod naturalis ratio subserviat fidei* (I, 1, 8 ad 2). Besides, is it at possible to

synthesis, he did not take this doctrine into account? Why is there scarcely an allusion found there to the theme of the imitation of Christ? And for all that St. Thomas was convinced of the utility, of the necessity even, of moral exemplarism. In fact he wrote in the *Contra Gentiles*: *we are incited to virtue both by words and by example.*[24] He prefers the truth to mere fictions and to edifying fables or pious legends.[25] Would he not much prefer the *total exemplar* of a person who "speaks" to another person, to the individual and singular traits found in the immense literature of *examples, exempla?*

---

avoid a certain use of philosophy? We should recall in this regard the paradoxical reflection of K. BARTH, *Die kirchl. Dogmatik*, 1, 2, ed. 4, Zürich 1948, pp. 815 ff. According to Barth, no interpreter of Scripture can be satisfied with simply making observations on it and expounding; of necessity he thinks *with* the Scripture and *on the basis* of Scripture. Consciously or not, he comes to the sacred text with a certain knowledge, with a logic, with a conception of the world and of the relations between God and the world. The exegesis of Ch. Baur would be inconceivable without the philosophy of Hegel; the *Formegeschichte* without the phenomenology of Husserl. Consequently, the interpreter of the Bible must of necessity make "use" of some philosophy or other. Only, for Barth, this necessity is a consequence of the fact that nature is corrupted by sin, whereas for St. Thomas this necessity derives from a completely opposite source: nature and reason are not totally corrupted by sin.

But St. Thomas never confuses his "expositions" of the philosophical order with the "authority" of Scripture. Cf. II Sent., dist. 14, q. 1, a 2: *Expositores Sacrae Scripturae in hoc diversificati sunt, secundum quod diversorum philosophorum sectatores fuerunt.* But the Fathers of the Church, when they use a system of philosophy of their choice, *non sunt maioris auctoritatis quam dicta philosophorum quae sequuntur, nisi in hoc quod sunt ab omni infidelitatis suspicione separati.* Could St. Thomas have had a different opinion about *his own* references to philosophy?

24. *IV Contra Gentiles*, c. 54, 6°.

25. Opusc. 12 (Ad lect. Bisuntinum): Non decet praedicatorem veritatis ad *fabulas* ignotas devertere.

It is precisely in reference to this total and personal exemplar that he remarks, not without a certain delicacy, that the more the moral exemplar is held in *esteem*, the more it is the object of our appreciation and good opinion, the greater influence does it exercise.[26] The practical effectiveness of the model depends, in consequence of this, in large measure on a judgment of "value" which we pass on it.

But all human models, just as all human words, are fallible. We cannot set up for ourselves the perfect exemplar for which we are looking. Hence the fittingness of the *Incarnation*, which offers to us an infallible and unfailing model of life, and a moral teaching which can contain no error.[27] A new light is thrown on every single aspect of the moral life by this most important event. Through the Incarnation the possibility of the beatific vision becomes manifest for us.[28] As the support of our hope the Incarnation frees us from the anguish of sin.[29] Convincing us of man's true dignity in that God did not disdain to assume our nature, the Incarnation teaches

---

26. *IV C.G.*, c. 54, 6°: exempla alicuius et verba tanto efficacius ad virtutem inducunt, quanto de eo *firmior bonitatis habetur opinio.*

27. *Ibid.*: unde necessarium fuit homini ad hoc quod in virtute firmaretur, quod a Deo humanato doctrinam et exempla virtutis acciperet.

28. *Ibid.*, 1. It is a question here of an *a fortiori* argument. If God was able to unite to himself, *in unitate personae*, a human nature, with much greater reason can one conclude that it is not impossible (*evidentissime demonstratur*) that the created intellect be united to God in the act of vision (*quod homo per intellectum Deo potest uniri*).

29. *Ibid.*, 7°.

the inanity and emptiness of idolatry and of the worship of animals.[30] It enlightens and nurtures our faith,[31] it calls forth in us the movement of love and of charity,[32] and opens up to us the secret of divine friendship.[33]

This most important chapter of the *Contra Gentiles* could well have constituted the basis and context of a moral theology organized entirely on the principle of exemplarism, of the imitation of Christ. Its essential elements are to be found again in the *Summa Theologica*, when St. Thomas treats of the mysteries of Christ's life.[34]

THE "TERTIA PARS" AND MORAL THEOLOGY

All the texts of the Tertia Pars that are of interest for moral theology can be grouped around the fundamental distinction of imitation already indicated above. A certain number emphasize the notion of imitation in the ontological sense (*to be* in imitation of . . .). Thus, our adoption is appropriated to the Father as to its author, to the Son as to its exemplar.[35] The predestination of Christ is "the exemplar" of ours,[36] the Resurrection of

---

30. *Ibid.*, 3°.
31. *Ibid.*, 3°.
32. *Ibid.*, 4°.
33. *Ibid.*, 6°.
34. Cf. A. VAN KOL, *Christus' Plaats in S. Thomas Moraalsysteem*, Roermond 1947, pp. 95-97.
35. III, q. 23, a. 2 ad 3.
36. III, q. 24, a. 4.

Christ is the exemplar of our future resurrection,[37] and in the present life, it is the exemplar of our spiritual resurrection.[38]

A much greater number of texts have to do with imitation in the moral sense of the term (*to act in* imitation of ...): Christ was offered to men as an example or model in all things,[39] as example of patience,[40] of prayer,[41] of humility,[42] of obedience.[43] Christ wished to be tempted by the devil in order to show us how we must resist him.[44] In his passion Christ offers himself to us as the perfect model of all the virtues.[45]

Notwithstanding all that, the influence of Christ as exemplar of the moral life is not limited, in the thought of St. Thomas, to the imitation of the virtues and of the actions of Christ. There is in Christ something which we are capable of imitating immediately in this life: his patience, his gentleness, his humility. Other elements can be imitated by us only in an *eschatological* sense: our future resurrection *will be* an imitation of the Resurrection of Christ. Then, there is something which cannot be imitated by us, neither in the present life nor eschato-

---

37. III, q. 54, a. 2.
38. III, q. 56, a. 2.
39. III, q. 39, a. 3 ad 3; cf. q. 40, a. 1 ad 3; a. 2 ad 1; q. 41, a. 2 ad 1.
40. III, q, 14, a. 1.
41. III, q. 21, a. 1, a. 2, a. 3, a. 4 ad 1.
42. III, q. 37, a. 3 ad 2; q. 40, a. 3, ad 3.
43. III, q. 37, a. 1; a. 3 ad 3.
44. III, q. 41, a. 1; a. 4 ad 6.
45. III, q. 46, a. 3.

logically in the future. And here I mean the stupendous fact of the *Incarnation*. We are not, nor shall we ever be sons of God by nature, as Christ is. And for all that, this important event exercises a decisive influence on our moral life, in a special way on the life and activity of the theological virtues, virtues that constitute that which is most perfect in us and that which is, in the most proper sense of the term, "Christians." For the Incarnation gives to our faith a *certitude* which it would certainly never have had without it. The Incarnation raises and strengthens our hope; nothing more than it is capable of arousing in us love and charity. The importance of Christology, then, for ethics or moral theology, is not to be restricted exclusively to the theme of the "imitation" of Christ. Beyond the life and actions of Christ, we should, as the mystics recommend, raise ourselves up to Christ himself.[46]

The moral teaching of St. Thomas is not just a moral theology of virtues and of duties; it is continued into and receives its completion from *contemplation*. The two aspects which must be distinguished in this thorny question concerning the relation between "Christology" and "Moral theology" can, as a consequence of what has

---

46. Here it would be necessary to study in particular three texts in which St. Thomas distinguishes explicitly these two aspects: the life of Christ as exemplar of the life of the virtues, and the profound depths of the mystery the contemplation of which should call fourth in us the intensity of the acts of the theological virtues. Cf. III, q. 1, a. 2; q. 46, a. 3; q. 53, a. 1.

just been said, be attached on the one hand to the active life, and on the other to the contemplative life. The imitation of the virtues and actions of Christ is founded above all on the first, on the active life. It is the peculiar characteristic of contemplation to attain to *the high-set caverns from the rocks below,*[47] as St. John of the Cross puts it.

It is manifest, then, that the Tertia Pars furnishes us with all the elements of a moral theology and its prolongation, mystical theology, both of them authentically integrated into Christology. We may well ask why such a point of view is missing from the vast synthesis of moral theology set up in the I-II and the II-II of the *Summa Theologica?*[48]

---

47. Cantico Espiritual, canto 37. Here the saint explains that the rock from which or through which one ascends to the sublime and profound mysteries of the wisdom of God is none other than Christ and a life lived in imitation of his example, in the exercise of the Christian virtues that make up the active life.

48. The all-important text of *I Cor.* 11, 1 is never quoted in the two Summas. *I Cor.* 4, 16 on the contrary is quoted five times (see above all II-II, q. 2, a. 6 ad 3 and q. 43, a. 5). *John* 13, 34 is also quoted four times. The only interesting text is to be found in I-II, 68, a. 1: In this text St. Thomas is refuting the opinion of Philip the Chancellor concerning the distinction between the virtues and the gifts: *Alii vero ... dixerunt quod virtutes ordinantur simpliciter ad bene operandum, sed dona ordinantur ad hoc quod per ea conformemur Christo, praecipue quantum ad ea quae passus est. ... Sed hoc etiam non videtur esse sufficiens. Quia ipse Dominus praecipue nos inducit ad sui conformitatem secundum mansuetudinem ... et secundum caritatem* (John 13, 34 quoted). *Et hae etiam virtutes praecipue in passione Christi refulserunt.*

V The Principles of "Personal Exemplarity" and the Thought of St. Thomas

St. Thomas was fully convinced of the necessity of concrete examples in the teaching of moral theology: we are incited to virtue both by word and by example. But the systematic use of examples and of concrete facts or events is, for him, above all the business of preaching: it is a preacher's business to propose the good deeds of others as examples to be followed.[1] Now, according to his mind preaching is not the same thing as sacred science, as theology, although both of them, again as he saw things, should flow from the fullness of contemplation.[2] Consequently, as an integral part of sacred science, the moral theology of St. Thomas does not aim at being a "theology of preaching," a direct exhortation to the practice of the virtues. And for that reason it is not its concern to carry through the principle of adducing examples, which is nothing else than a type of exhortatory

---

1. *I Thess.* 1, 7; St. Thomas, lect. 1, n° 19.
2. II-II, q. 188, a. 6.

method.[3] To act otherwise would be to substitute the rhetorical art for science, for the science of morals.[4]

But here we must be careful to distinguish carefully between two things. It is one thing to speak of examples, particular and limited in scope, and quite a different thing altogether to speak of a "person-exemplar" (*Vorbild*), of a person that presents itself (or is presented) to the disciple, who "follows" it, who walks in its footsteps, as a total model of life and living, as a model that claims, on the part of the disciple, a total involvement, and a total adhesion. Is it possible to find a place for the "principle of personal exemplarity," for the *Vorbildsprinzip*, in the moral synthesis of St. Thomas Aquinas?

Let us first of all consider the human act, as St.

---

3. In Prol. Sent. a. 5: Ad tria proceditur in Sacra Scriptura, scilicet ad destructionem errorum . . . et ideo oportet modum huius scientiae esse quandoque argumentativum. . . . Proceditur etiam *ad instructionem morum*: unde quantum ad hoc, modus eius debet esse *praeceptivus*, sicut in lege, *comminatorius et promissivus*, ut in prophetis, et *narrativus exemplorum*, ut in historialibus. Proceditur tertio ad contemplationem veritatis, sicut in quaestionibus Sacrae Scripturae et ad hoc oportet modum etiam esse argumentativum.—Between the apologetic function of the "sacra doctrina" and the literature of the "questions," St. Thomas perceives a moral teaching which could well be called homiletic in type, a teaching that formulates precepts, promises and menaces and which also offers *examples* of virtues to be imitated. In the first question of the Summa Theologica (I, q. 1) there is no trace of this homiletic type of moral teaching. To find some allusion to the "modi" of which it can make use one must go to the tract on Law (cf. I-II, q. 92, a. 2; q. 99, a. 6).

4. ST. THOMAS, In Post. Anal., I, lect. 1, n. 12: in rhetoricis persuasio fit . . . per *exemplum*, non autem per syllogismum aut per inductionem completam.

Thomas does in the tract *on Human Acts*, in its singularity and individuality. Are we to believe that every human *act*, every moral act, demands necessarily the intervention of a *personal model*, which the human agent intends to imitate in his conduct? The answer to this cannot be in the affirmative. St. Thomas never thinks of the human act without an object, without an end, without circumstances, amongst which circumstances one will seek in vain for a circumstance entitled: *according to the example of*. On the other hand, there is neither moral goodness nor moral evil without a relation of conformity to or of disagreement with, "reason," or "Eternal Law." In all this there is no trace to be found of the "person-model," nor of the essential place it would hold in the structure of the moral life.

But matters change altogether if, instead of considering the human act in isolation and in all its individuality, we seek to examine *the totality of a human life* and its complete development, which finds in death its total fulfillment and its limit. For death is the "end of being in the world." This end, which belongs essentially to existence, to the very possibility of being, limits and determines the total possibility "of being in the world."[5] A human life, considered thus in its totality, is subjected to

5. M. HEIDEGGER, *Sein und Zeit*, ed. 7, pp. 233-234. Needless to say the Christian mind understands the "Sein zum Tode" in a completely different sense to that of the existentialism of Heidegger.

the condition that man is by nature an "animal sociale." It is in one and in many simultaneous social ambients that man manifests in time the virtualities of his power of action. The moral life is lived *amongst others*, sometimes in concord with them, sometimes in antagonism to them. In this way the human agent finds round about him personal models from which he just cannot abstract. It is thus that the old Aristotelian principle, *man is by nature a social being*, enables us to make place for the doctrine of moral exemplarism. On the other side, one must take into account the importance of the doctrine of *friendship* in thomistic moral teaching. In true friendship, that namely founded on the common possession of virtue, one friend becomes for the other an authentic model of virtue. Here, too, we come again upon the place of exemplarism and imitation in the moral teaching of St. Thomas.

These remarks refer above all to ethics, to moral philosophy. But what about theology, moral theology? The "second dimension," which we envisaged above in human activity, is not entirely absent from the *Summa* of St. Thomas. The huge treatise on the virtues and the gifts, which begins with question 55 of the I-II, has the equivalent to offer us. While an act passes in an instant, the virtuous life demands a temporal dimension, which coincides in fact with the totality of each one's life. Now, the virtuous life does not consist only in the regular exercise of the moral and of the "political" virtues. Over and above that it is an invitation to man to raise himself up to the divine life: *to raise himself up to divine things in so far as that is possible.*[6] Adopting the plotinian theory of virtues, which he knew through Macrobius,[7] St. Thomas is in that way able to make place for the "imitation" of the exemplar virtues, as they are in God. The first are, properly speaking, the virtues of the soul on the way towards purification; the latter belong to the soul already "purified" by contemplation. It is of the soul already purified that we can above all say: *he is united to the mind of God by an unending pact in so far, namely, as he imitates it.*[8] But with the Greeks it was a question of imitating an "Idea." In Christian language it is a question of imitating the "living" God, who manifested himself in history. One would have welcomed it had St. Thomas stressed with greater force this difference. However that may be, we need not examine further the I-II in order to find there the imitation of Christ, the imitation of the Passion of Christ.[9] And there we have already the herald of the vast christological exemplarism which we analysed above.

---

6. ST. THOMAS, I-II, q. 61, a. 5.

7. In reality Macrobius depends more on Porphyry than on Plotin. Cf. H. VAN LIESHOUT, *La doctrine plotinienne de la vertu,* Studia Fribur-gensia 5, Fribourg-Paderborn-Paris 1926, p. 117.

8. I-II, q. 61, a. 5.

9. See note Chap. 4, note 47 above.

ACT, PERSON AND "OPTION"

It would never have occurred to St. Thomas to say, as Goethe did, "that in the beginning was action," but he does think that that which does not act is not, does not exist. Now, to act, just as to be, is not the quality of ideas nor of abstract natures, but rather of *concrete subjects*. The human act, it too is seen to be the property of the person: *action has its source, not in nature, but in the person*.[10] Authentic human acts, then, acts that are truly the object of consideration by moral science, are acts of the "person."

If we strive to get beyond the letter while remaining true to the spirit of St. Thomas' work, the following distinction can be proposed. It is one thing to speak of acts of the *person* (all human acts are comprised in this) and quite another thing to speak of absolutely *personal* acts in the strictest sense of that term. In the ordinary run of daily human life we place many acts that are truly human and free, but in and through which the person is not totally involved or engaged. On the contrary, that act is in a supreme degree personal in which a man, having "deliberated" about what "he wishes to do with himself," ordains his whole life to a concrete final end, that act, namely, by which he determines *the scope or pur-*

---

10. ST. THOMAS, In ad Rom., c. 1, lect. 3.

pose of his life, the very meaning of his existence.[11] To
wish the good in general, to desire "felicity" or happiness
and its peaceful and undisturbed possession, these are
the constants of man's nature.[12] On the contrary, to
make of such and such a good the end, the scope or goal
of one's life, that is a determination, an absolutely personal "option," that is the business of the person, of
John or Peter or Paul.

We should not think that this decisive option is the
prerogative of great personalities, of illustrious minds, or
of famous converts. No man, however ordinary his culture may be or however limited his intelligence, could
ever hope to escape it. Take a man of medium culture
and education and brought up in the Christian faith.
Suddenly, one day, he rejects as a texture of legends
and fables the faith of his childhood. He may doubtlessly
have certain partial excuses, which others may not have:
the influence of his social ambient, the absence of a deep
religious culture or training. He has, nonetheless, made
a decisive option concerning the "scope" of his life and
of his own existence.

This decisive option, this supremely personal act, is it
performed in reference to a person? If this be the case,
then the dilemma might be put in these terms: either "to

---

11. I-II, q. 89, a. 6.
12. I-II, q. 1, a. 7 ad 3; *Ver.*, q. 22, a. 7.

DARLINGTON SEMINARY LIBRARY
DARLINGTON, N. J. 07446

follow" this person and become his disciple, or reject it and seek other masters. Here the answer is at one and the same time both simple and very complex. If we dealing with a subject to whom divine Revelation has been sufficiently proposed, that is, of someone who has been sufficiently instructed in the truths of the Christian faith, then without any doubt the answer is in the affirmative. Either there is the *worship of faith*, which is the adhering to the Person of Christ, and, through Him and in Him, to the Father and the Holy Spirit; or there is refusal purely and simply. Acceptance or refusal of Christ who speaks to us through the medium of the Church's ministry, that is the fundamental option which separates the Christian from the unbeliever.

But what are we to think of those who are invincibly ignorant of the Gospel of Christ, of those who have in no way been attained by the Church's preaching? The Church teaches the almost infinitely consoling doctrine, that the way of salvation is not closed to them. For those who "observe the natural law and its precepts, and show themselves disposed to be obedient to God in leading an upright and honest life, can attain to eternal life under the active influence of divine light and divine grace."[13] Through the lights and inspirations of internal grace, those who have not had the benefit of the

---

13. Encyc. "Quanto conficiamur moerore," 10 August 1863, Denzs 2866; cf. Decr. of Holy Office, 8 August 1949, AER 127 (1952) 30.

HARRINGTON SEMINARY LIBRARY
BRIGHTON & MASS.

preached word can, in view of what has been said, attain to justification and ultimately to eternal salvation.

But what about the others? About those in the immense pagan masses have not in fact arrived at justification under the mysterious action of divine interior grace, have they all positively sinned against the faith? Have they all refused that immediate and proximate internal help which would have enabled them to attain directly to faith and to justification? St. Thomas did not think so and only very few theologians have made their own the contrary opinion. Side by side with what are called positive infidels, who reject the faith either by formal active rejection or refusal, or by simple omission, St. Thomas recognized the presence of purely *negative*[14] infidels, who are *excused* from the sin of infidelity by the *invincible ignorance* in which they find themselves with respect to the preaching of the Gospel. Finally, if they are damned, that will be for the other sins which they may have committed against the natural law and not for the sin of infidelity which could not be imputed to them.

This presupposes that the *first* object of option which presents itself to all men[15] is not the very object of faith

---

14. ST. THOMAS, II-II, q. 10, a. 1.
15. St. Thomas is of the opinion that this option between the good and the evil must be made from the first instant of the use of reason (I-II, q. 89, a. 6). But his opinion is far from being universally accepted.

itself, the living God, Providence, Remuneration.[16] Were this not the case, then there could never be question of admitting the existence of purely negative infidels. Consequently we are lead to asserting that the first object of option is constituted by the *Natural Law*, the choice between good and evil, a choice that is presented quite obviously not in an abstract fashion, but in a concrete context, that namely of a certain action to be placed or of a certain evil to be avoided. Those who (with the help of actual grace) path of good, those God will lead to the act of faith and to justification. Those who the way of evil will have sinned against the *Natural Law* directly, but not directly against the faith, for the simple reason that the object of faith was not yet proposed to them. And for that reason they have not at all committed the formal sin of infidelity.

According to this analysis it should be clear that the first option is not an "answer" of person to person, but appears rather as *obedience to a law*, to the natural law, which speaks through the voice of conscience. It may perhaps be objected that in order to know the existence of a law that binds me I must first of all know *the existence and the authority of the Legislator*, who promul-

---

16. Modern theologians are unanimous in demanding explicit faith in the two first *credibilia* only: *Deum esse et Remuneratorem*, of those to whom the Gospel was never in any way offered by external preaching. As to the mysteries of the Trinity and of the Redemptive Incarnation implicit faith suffices (Suarez) or explicit faith "in voto" (Salmanticenses).

gated it. The knowledge of the natural law and the instigation of conscience would, in this case, seem to suppose the *explicit* knowledge of God, the sovereign Legislator. And the more we extend the possibility of *invincible ignorance* of the existence of God in the case of man left to himself (that is, without the help of Revelation), the more possible will it be that there exist, in vast sectors of the human race, individuals who are "adults by age, but not by reason" (L. Billot), that is, individuals who are hindered by the invincible ignorance of God from arriving at the threshold of moral conscience. But this doctrine, that of the "limbo for adults," never got a large number of adherents. One could, however, quite well reason the other way about and believe that, on the contrary, the knowledge of the moral law and the voice of conscience enable us to argue back to the existence of the sovereign Legislator of morality.[17] In any event, as we saw above (chapter II), two quite different things must be carefully distinguished: on the one hand, the knowledge more or less confused of a personal God, a knowledge which must be presupposed to the knowledge of the moral law; and on the other hand,

---

17. Cf. D. BANEZ, comm. ad II-II, q. 10, a. 1, dub. II: "Quamvis tunc —in the instant of coming to the use of reason—invincibiliter ignoret homo Deum esse *explicite,* non tamen inde sequitur quod non obligetur lege naturali Dei, quia talis lex repraesentatur homini ab ipsa synderesi, vices Dei gerente et obligante. *Ex qua obligatione quam ipse homo experitur, poterit postea demonstrari Deum esse supremum iudicem:* ... me naturaliter obligari sentio ..., ergo superiorem habeo."

that personal "encounter," that direct and intimate relation to the living God, which is demanded by the moral theology of the *Nachfolge*. This is an encounter and personal involvement which is the foundation for an immediate personal relationship, which we, on the contrary, find in faith, as will be seen later (chapter VI).

ST. THOMAS AQUINAS AND PERSONALISM[18]

St. Thomas affirmed the excellence and superiority of the person in a famous text: *it is the most sublime thing in all of nature*,[19] but he immediately adds: *subsisting in a rational nature*. It is in no way the intention of St. Thomas to oppose the axiological content, the dignity of the *person* to the dignity of the intellectual *nature*. Quite the contrary: it is from the intellectual and individual *nature* present in it that the person derives its dignity. As every conscience or consciousness is the conscience or consciousness of some particular thing, as the phenomenologists have taught us, in no lesser way is the person that what it is uniquely because it is a *human*, *angelic* or *divine* person. The getting rid of ethics or moral philosophy in the common and popular sense of the term, that is, the ethics of "human nature," in the

---

18. Cf. L. B. Gillon, O.P., *La morale di S. Tommaso e il Personalismo*, Sap 1952, 1-8.

19. ST. THOMAS, I, q. 29, a. 3.

name of the higher and purely individual values of the person, can, in virtue of what we have said, have no meaning in thomistic thought.

St. Thomas would have vigorously rejected that extreme form of personalism which denies every subjection of the person to any law whatsoever, and that in the name of the superior dignity or nobility of the person itself. In this case we would not be far removed from the medieval errors of the "Brethren of the Free Spirit," nor from those of the "Enlightened" ("Illuminati") of the 16th century, who fell foul of the Spanish Inquisition. Only God, declare the false mystics, can command the children of God. Against all these tendencies, we must remember that the Church, just as all political and domestic societies and all legitimately constituted superiors, whatever their title may otherwise be, has the power to order or command men; it can make them the object of *precepts*, which bind them in conscience.

But the question which interests us is more subtle. Is it necessary that the law, which is by definition universal and common, first of all become an individual precept before the person feel itself truly bound by it? Has the human person really the right to make this dialectical transformation of the common and universal law into an absolutely individual precept the condition of its obedience? The solution to these questions depends on the manner one conceives of the relations between "person" and "nature." If the person is "part" of a nature, then the law imposed by God on human nature, the "natural" law, binds it immediately in so far as it is included *in* this very nature, and the dialectical transposition, of which we spoke, is no longer universally necessary. One must reason in the same way in the case of family or domestic authority, of political society, indeed of every other "authority," making the reservations, however, demanded by the fact of belonging to these several different social groups. For man is not entirely "part" of political society, he is not part of it totally and according to every aspect of his being.[20] However, if it be false to say that the person cannot be bound immediately by a law, in as far as it is universal and has for object a "community" of which the person is a "part," it is for all that true that the personal precept implies a fullness of efficacy, and a dynamic force which the abstract and universal law does not possess.

THE PRINCIPLE OF PERSONAL EXEMPLARITY

We know already that this famous principle does not consist entirely in recommending the use of concrete examples in the teaching of moral science, nor even in simply presenting the example of some great personality,

20. I-II, q. 21, a. 4 ad 3.

of some hero, or genius, or saint, to be for the disciple a concrete model of life. In this sense the principle of personal exemplarity has a very obvious value. That no one denies.

What we are getting at is reducible to this: does the understanding and grasping of "values" and moral norms suppose in the subject the adhering through love to a "person-model," which possesses these values and fulfills these norms in an eminent degree? If so, then, put into thomistic terminology, this means that the *first fundamental principle* of the moral life is precisely the person-model, and the adhering to it in love. Now, quite manifestly all this is quite foreign to the thought of St. Thomas. The *first principle* of the moral life, is not for him a person, but rather a *precept: the good is to be done, evil is to be avoided*, a double assertion which must be understood both of good and evil, not only in the order of appetibility, but also in that of morality.[21] In other words, the starting point of morality for the Angelic Doctor, does not consist in the adhering to a "person of value," but in the knowledge and adhering or involvement which is rooted in the first principles of the "natural law."

Now, in the language of Kant, the principle of personal exemplarity means that the "respect" of the Law

21. I-II, q. 94, a. 2.

supposes the "respect" of the person who promulgates the Law. But what happens when the legislator is not altogether worthy of respect, when he is not a "person of value"? Would we, in that case, be dispensed from obeying a person whom we could not respect? Catholic moralists do not think so. It is sufficient that the law be made by a *legitimate authority* and that it be in itself *just*, for we are bound to obey even the evil and the godless.

On the other hand we must be careful not to confuse the "pre-moral" life of children with the true moral life. "The child of 5-7 years, scarcely arrived at the use of reason and judgment, has a knowledge of the moral norms; but at that age the norm which teaches the moral good is accepted as long as it is proposed by the parents or by any person whatever invested with the authority of an adult. . . . At about 10-12 years children affirm their own moral responsibility, their own uprightness, not only because this is affirmed and taught by others . . . , but because they realize it themselves and are conscious of it. A more decided differentiation is found in adolescents and youths."[22] As A. Gemelli further remarks, with the appearance of the moral sense, the child is in possession of a *subjective* criterion of value, and he does not wait to receive quite passively from others, from the parents or teachers, the distinction between good and evil. Were

22. A. GEMELLI, *La psicologia dell 'età evolutiva*, ed. 5, Milan 1956, pp. 332-333.

one to push forward or emphasize too much the principles of the moral teaching based on the *Nachfolge*,
would one not arrive at a morality infantile in character,
like the one we have just described?

Man is capable of waxing enthusiastic for abstract
ideal, as for instance, for justice, for Communism etc.,
and of making of them the goal of his life. In the case
of adults, all this does not presuppose necessarily the
preliminary adhering through love to the person of value
that is representative of this abstract ideal. Do all faithful Communists have this preliminary attachment to the
person of K. Marx? That could not be answered in the
affirmative. But with that we have said enough about
the philosophical problem raised by a consideration of
the principle of personal exemplarity.

THE IMITATION OF CHRIST

The Christian life, on the contrary, seems to be in a
position to give to the morality of the *Nachfolge* that
meaning and significance which we hesitate to attribute
to it on the philosophical level alone. Is not the Christian
life above all an unconditioned attachment to the *Person*
of Christ by means of faith, hope and charity? The
practice of the virtues, obedience to the precepts of
Christ and the Church, everything flows from that. In
this attachment then to a person that "speaks" to us

we would seem to have re-discovered the fundamental postulate of the morality of personal imitation.

It is necessary, however, to point out clearly and insistently that this total commitment to the following of Christ, this "encounter," and this attachment, should not be regarded as implying the *irrational* character which our contemporaries are only too inclined to attribute to them. According to the teaching of the Church, the act of faith is *reasonable* and the abandon or commitment which it involves does not do away with the necessity of a certain assessment of the motives of credibility, as assessment which is different in each one.[23]

Instead of the abstract rule: act in accordance with reason, the following concrete rule is offered to us: do that which Christ did (or would do) in your "situation." Such a rule of action is in itself excellent, though it did call forth certain reactions (see above, chapter I). In any case, it is all-important to note that that which Christ did, that which he prescribes for us and that of which he shows himself the incomparable model, all that cannot be reduced to one single plane. The first Vatican Council obliges us to distinguish *"in rebus divinis"* (in matters pertaining to God) two distinct levels of truth: on the one hand, mysteries properly so-called, that are absolutely inaccessible to reason; and on the other hand, certain

---

23. Encyc. "Qui pluribus," 9 Nov. 1846, DenzS 2778; conc. Vat. I, Const. de Fide, can. 3, DenzS 3033.

truths that are not inaccessible to it, although God deigned to make them known to us through his word of revelation.[24] One cannot avoid making the same distinction in the order of the moral virtues. We are absolutely obliged to distinguish on one side, that which Scheler called the "sacred," that is, "revealed" morality, the theological order, and on the other side, the natural law. The natural law has indeed been taken up by Christ and brought to perfection, but we could not ever admit that knowledge of it and a certain imperfect carrying out of its precepts *always and everywhere* presuppose an attachment to Christ in love. To maintain such a position would be tantamount to falling into a kind of *moral fideism* and to denying every possibility of morally good acts, from the "natural" point of view (that is, non-meritorious acts), either to pagans, who have never in any way had a knowledge of the Gospel, or to unbelievers. But such a position is rejected by the Church.[25]

It will doubtlessly be said that this distinction between the natural law and the strictly supernatural precepts has indeed a certain value from the "essentialist" and abstract point of view, but that the Christian, placed as he is under the direction of the Law of Christ, adheres in one single movement or impetus, both to the revealed mysteries and to the ethical consequences which they

24. DenzS 3005; 3015.
25. DenzS 1925; 1927; 1935; 2438-2439; 2623.

imply, and to the precepts of the natural law. From the existential point of view, while the real difference between the two is not denied, no distinction or separation can be admitted or even conceived. Life unites that which analysis divides and separates. For the Christian there is only one morality and only one Law, the Law of Christ. The Christian acts only for Christ and that is the meaning and the demand of the formula of St. Paul: *in Christ Jesus*. To teach and admit that is not to deny the existence, for pagans and unbelievers, of a certain imperfect natural morality, which does not quite presuppose this fundamental attachment to Christ.

Such an explanation is true if we understand it from the point of view of the *end*, but it is not true if understood from the point of view of the *object*. Every human act implies both the one and the other together. Let us take any most ordinary act of everyday life, the buying of a railway-ticket, for example. We can perform it for a most exalted end, for a "supernatural" end, as, for instance, to carry out an act of the sacred ministry, or to keep a vow taken to make a pilgrimage. It is nonetheless true that this act, in itself, by reason of the *object*, which specifies it immediately and by reason of the simple act of justice that it implies, is not at all *immediately and intrinsically supernatural*, as would be an act of prayer, an act of faith or an act of charity. And for that reason we teach the Christian to raise up, always and everywhere, his "intention" to Christ, to do everything for Christ, *in Christo Jesu*. But this lofty intention, which is realized completely and fully only in those souls that have reached divine union, can in no way do away with the specific distinction of *objects*. And this is not just to consider the abstract "essence," but rather to take into account the very existential structure of human acts.

To proclaim the existence of the natural law and the binding force of positive law does not entail falling into that "legalism" which is so discredited today. The legalistic spirit knows nothing but laws, the precept. It is ignorant and unaware of the spontaneity inherent in the glad gift of love. St. Thomas has warned us against this danger of legalism when writing his magnificent tract on the New Law. "That which is of greatest importance in the Law of the New Testament," he writes, "is *the grace of the Holy Spirit*, which is given to us through faith in Christ. The New Law is as a consequence first and foremost the grace of the Holy Spirit."[26] Such a Law is not written on tables of stone, as was the law of Moses, but in the hearts of men. The Law of the New Testament is in the first place an *interior* law and it is for that reason that it is identified with grace. Has it, then, done away with every external element, with every

---

26. ST. THOMAS, I-II, q. 106, a. 1.

kind of precept and all external rite? Obviously not. But it is only in second place, although still in a *necessary and essential* way,[27] that the New Law is also, in its own way, a written law, an external law, a series of precepts and a body of rites surrounding the seven sacraments, those means which God normally employs to accord us his grace, his interior grace which is the very first substantial element of the New Law.

---

27. The words of St. Thomas: *quasi secundaria* do not mean that the external precepts and the obedience due to them, the sacraments etc., are something accidental in the new economy of salvation, and something left to the choice of each, but rather something that comes in second place, while being all the essential.

VI The Integration of Moral Theology Into Christology

In this connection a preliminary question must be asked: is it a matter of integrating moral theology into Christology or rather Christology into moral theology? It is not the same thing. Let us explain these two hypotheses.

Moral theology is regarded today as a science completely distinct from dogmatic theology, in much the same way that ethics is distinct from metaphysics or from psychology. Now, the concept of integration and that of autonomy are absolutely *contradictory*. To be "integrated" means to lose one's autonomy or independence. Should one wish to the fully autonomous *state* of moral theology as a science, then the problem of its integration into Christology has no meaning. But, for all that, there is nothing to stop it becoming "edifying," of coming nearer to "spiritual theology"; nor is there anything to stop introducing Christ into it, the person of Christ as the perfect model of the moral life, whom Christians should "follow." In all this it is obviously more a question of *superimposing* a certain number of new elements on a moral theology that is fundamentally classical, rather than of a *total re-casting*, a re-modelling from the very foundations, that would transform it radically.

In the very other extreme, integration could be understood in a quite unorthodox sense. It would have such a sense were one to assign as its basis the ontological identity of the activity of a Christian and that of Christ.[1] The Christian *is* Christ, the action of a Christian *is* the action of Christ. One arrives in that way at an ultra-realistic interpretation of the doctrine of the Mystical Body, the consequence of which is that very distinction between moral theology and Christology. In that case, moral theology is nothing more and can be nothing more than a Christology; it is, in fact, Christology *tout court*.

In St. Thomas the problem is put in quite different terms, for the simple reason that he taught the fundamental *unity* of all theology. His moral theology is not a distinct and separate and independent science. We saw already that the III Pars contains all the elements of a moral theology *integrated* into Christology. But this moral theology of the III Pars is not the moral theology of St. Thomas, because it *presupposes as already carried out and made one's own the ontological analysis of the*

---

1. The following assertion is attributed to Almaricus of Bene: *Pater incarnatus est in Abraham . . . Filius in Christo et in christianis* (*Contra Amaurianos*, ed. Bauemker, BGPTMA 24, 5-6, p. 30). See also M. T. D'ALEVNY, *Un fragment du procès des Amauriciens*, AHD 25-26 (1950-1951) 325-336.

various structures, of which it is question: faith, hope, charity, the moral virtues. And this ontological analysis has been carried out with great care in the vast treatises of the I-II and the II-II.

With regard to this last point, it was the manifest intention of St. Thomas to gather together in one sole *ensemble* all the questions pertaining to moral theology found here and there in the text of the Sentences of Peter Lombard. There are in fact in the Sentences two distinct groups of questions dealing with moral theology: in book II, distinction 23-44, and book III, distinction 23-40. In a certain sense, these are the two poles around which are built up the I-II and the II-II. There were, then, two possibilities open: either to gather together *all* moral theology after the Christology of the III Pars, and this would have had the advantage of linking it up very closely with the tract on the sacraments; or, then, to attach it entirely to the group of moral questions already existing in the second book of the Sentences, where Peter Lombard, having spoken about creation, introduced the examination of original sin and grace, of free will and the morality of human acts. This is, by and large, what St. Thomas did. His moral theology is entirely attached to the tract on creation and that on the divine government of the universe, and this he does by means of the notion of *image*.[2] St. Thomas' intention is to speak about

2. I-II, Prol.

the return to God of man, the image of God.[3] It is clear that image of which it is question here is above all the supernatural image: *image through the likeness of grace.*[4]

Now, an image cannot be understood except through its exemplar. If God as known to us even through revelation and faith ever remains over and above us in his transcendence, will it not be necessary here too to have recourse to the mediation of the Word made Flesh both in the order of knowledge and in that of action? In that case we will have got back to the perspectives of the commentary on 1 *Cor.* 11. Must we not regret the fact that St. Thomas did not adopt the other possibility or make the other contrary option and, taking inspiration from the other aspect of the plan of the Sentences, attach the whole group of 303 questions, which make up the moral part of his *Summa*, to the Christology of the III Pars? And here is a noteworthy confirmation of this: the tract on grace is an essential part of the moral theology of St. Thomas. But the grace of the New Testament is the grace of Christ. By detaching the tract on grace from Christology and by putting it beforehand in the plan of

---

3. This, from another point of view, does not in any way hinder God from being the "first subject" of the whole of sacred science. For human activity is not considered here except *in ordine ad Deum.* We will not go into the many discussions concerning the order of the different tracts in the Summa. The most recent study published on the matter may be mentioned: P. E. PEERSSON, *Le plan de la Somme Théologique et le rapport "ratio-revelatio,"* RPhL 56 (1958) 545-572.

4. I, 97, 4.

the *Summa,* has not St. Thomas emptied it of its true
meaning and character? More precisely, the structures of
the supernatural life are not just a series of participations
in the divine life, but are also participations in the plenitude of Christ, in the mysteries of the life of Christ. If
it be true that no participated thing can be understood
except through that of which it is a participation, then
from this point of view too we arrive at a strict sub-
ordination of moral theology to Christology.

GRACE, A SHARING IN THE PLENITUDE OF CHRIST

St. Thomas would admit this point without difficulty.
Of his fullness we have all received: in explaining these
words of St. John[5] he understands them without hesita-

---

5. Today one will reproach the thomistic doctrine of grace (which, let it
be said, on this precise point, has noting specifically "thomistic" about it)
with making of grace a "thing," a *static* gift, hidden in the depths of the
soul; it is, it will be said, tied up with the "fixist" concept of unchangeable
natures, a concept that has been abandoned by modern philosophy. It would
be better, today, to use the notions and insights of Personalism which would
give us a much more "dynamic" idea of grace. Grace is a gift from person
to person, a gift that calls for an answer of person to person. It is to
be placed in context of the "dialogue" between the I and the Thou (cf. K.
RAHNER, *Schriften z. Theologie,* I, 1954, p. 347; A. BRUNNER, *Eine neue
Schöpfung,* Paderborn 1952). In that way the doctrine of grace appears more
concrete, more vital, more "religious." It rids itself of the scholastic categories
of nature, habit and quality.

To this we answer that it is perfectly correct that grace is a gift, an
entitative "habit" (I-II, 50, 2). But this entitative gift, according to the
mind of St. Thomas, presupposes absolutely *uncreated grace,* the sovereign
gratuitous act of God's benevolence and love, who wishes to make of a
human being his friend, like unto Himself. It is precisely this benevolent will

tion of the *created* grace in Christ. He goes so far as to
say that Christ, as man, is in a certain sense the author
of grace, for he possesses in an absolute plenitude that
which we receive from him, the sharing in the life of
God.[6]

But it is not in the same sense that our grace is a
"participation" in the *fullness of the grace of Christ*, and
a "participation" in the divine nature, by which we be-

---

of God that constitutes the very *first* meaning of the word "grace" (I-II, q.
110, a. 1). Have we not, thus, rediscovered the "gift of the person," of the
divine Persons, which was demanded in the name of personalist philosophy?

Further it must be remembered that the gift of grace is not given by God
to an abstract nature. It is accorded to a concrete, existing *subject*. This subject, this human "person" is henceforward pleasing to God and acceptable to
him entirely. God considers him as an adoptive son. A particular, limited gift
does not render him to whom it is accorded absolutely good and perfect.
Grace, on the contrary, that heals (gratia sanans) and at the same time
elevates to life divine such a man, such a human subject, is an eminently
"personal" gift both from the point of view of its term and from that of
its principle. From now on the just man can "enjoy" the divine Persons
present within him by an ineffable mode of presence (I, q. 43, a. 3). It must
not be forgotten, however, that this intimate society, this "response" of man
to the absolutely gratuitous gift of God, presuppose that entitative, "static"
gift, that "habit" which one would so much like to get rid of. *How are we
to act as sons of God by adoption, if we are not first of all sons of God?* Act
and action follow on being and presuppose it. The just man acts as an adoptive son, because he *is* first of all an adoptive son: *filii Dei nominamur et
SUMUS.* This wonderful work that in the new creature, the *nova creatura,*
which is grace, must be accomplished first of all on the level of being. The
"entitative" habit of grace corresponds to this metaphysical necessity. But it
is in no way, nor does it pretend to be the *whole* of the supernatural life. It
is no more than its ontological base and principle, and vital principle at that,
since the entitative "habit" of grace is the radical principle of operation
(I-II, q. 111, a. 1).

6. ST. THOMAS, in John, 1, lect. 10.

come *sharers in the Divine nature* (*JJ Pet.* 1, 4). The created grace of Christ (it is not a question here of the grace of Union) is of the same nature as ours, exactly as the human nature of Christ is in everything like ours. Participation in this case, then, is found on the plane of *univocity*. In other words, it is a question of participation in a broad sense,[7] much in the same way as it can be said that every effect "participates" in its cause, through the actuation which it receives from it. To resume, then, it can be said that the grace of Christ is infinitely more perfect than ours by its quantity, by its "infinity"; but it is *of the same nature*: in him as in us it is a participation of the divine nature.

GRACE AS A SHARING IN THE DIVINE NATURE

Altogether different is the case of participation in the divine nature. Here no longer have to do with univocal participation, which requires that the thing or being which shares or is a sharing or participation of something else, and that in which it shares, should constitute a perfect ontological *identity*. We have to do, then, with *analogy*. God is the author of grace which gives us a new likeness to him, which has nothing in common with the gift of creation. But God is *infinitely above and superior*

---

7. *Ibid.*: De plenitudine eius partem aliquam *participamus* per ipsum.

to grace, even though this is truly a sharing in the very nature of God.[8]

Here, however, a precision which did not escape the keen insight of thomistic theologians must be made. Whereas grace, the virtues and the gifts are essentially "deiform" structures that form in us so many distinct principles of formal, though analogical, assimilation to the deity in all its depth, the sacramental characters, on the contrary, constitute for their part so many different principles of formal assimilation to the humanity of Christ.[9] Strictly speaking these are the "characters of

---

8. Cf. L. B. GEIGER, *La participation dans la philosophie de* Saint Thomas d'Aquin, Paris 1942, pp. 11-13. On the contrary, participation in the proper sense of the term, introduces us into analogy: *omne quod participatur determinatur ad modum participantis et sic partialiter habetur et non secundum omnem perfectionis modum* (Contra Gentiles I, c. 32). It belongs to man "by essence" (*essentialiter*) to be a rational animal; intelligence and being are not his except "by participation," in a *limited* way, different to the manner in which intelligence and being are in God (cf. In Col., c. 1, lect. 4). Let it also be added that, whereas man is also animal, he is not the *genus* of animal according to all the richness of that term, considered in the line of "intensive" abstraction. Cf. De Hebd., c. 2: *Homo dicitur participare animal, quia non habet rationem animalis secundum totam communitatem.* This is the "most complete" and the "most systematic" text that St. Thomas ever wrote on this matter. Cf. C. FABRO, *La nozione metafisica di partecipazione secondo S. Tommaso d'Aquino,* p. 15.

9. It can be said that our grace is like to that of Christ, that the created grace of Christ is like ours; it can also be said that our grace is like the deity, but *it is impossible to say that the deity is like grace.* In the first comparison a common *principle* is presupposed, in virtue of which the two terms are similar; in the second case we have a primal reality of which it cannot be said reciprocally that it is like something else. No one has expounded this distinction of the two similitudes more profoundly than Plotin, Enn., I, 2, 2. Through Denis this distinction came to the notice of St. Thomas, cf. I Sent., dist. 35, q. 1, a. 4 ad 6.

Christ,"[10] a participation in the priesthood which obviously belongs to Christ through his human, not through his divine nature.

An important conclusion follows from this. A moral theology, purporting to be essentially christological, *would, without any doubt whatever, have to take as its central theme, not the virtues or the precepts, but the sacramental characters*, and that would have the triple advantage of linking it up very closely with the priesthood of Christ, with the mystery of the Church and with the theology of the sacraments. Besides, these latter can all be linked up without much difficulty to the three sacramental characters. That would be by and large the plan of the moral theology of Hirscher (see chapter I).

St. Thomas would certainly have some difficulty in accepting this point of view. For him the character is essentially a "potency," a power, a physical power of acting or of being receptive. But one can use a power or a potency either well or ill. Consequently one cannot maintain that the character constitutes the principle of morality; it shows itself, on analysis, to be much rather

---

10. Cf. JOHN OF ST. THOMAS, *De sacramentis*, disp. XXV, a. 3: in exemplaritate et participatione character respicit sacerdotium Christi et consequenter Christum, secundum quod est homo, in quo differt a gratia quae est immediata participatio naturae divinae et ideo non respicit gratiam Christi aut Christum, secundum quod homo, in participatione et exemplaritate. Cf. also BANEZ, IIIam, ed. Beltran de Heredia, t. 2, Madrid 1935, p. 72.

an *exigency*, which can be met or satisfied only by
appealing to another principle, to *virtue* namely, which
in its turn flows from grace, grace itself being also an
effect of the sacraments, but an effect quite distinct
from the character. It is, then, virtue together with grace
which is presupposed to it and with the gifts of the
Holy Spirit which complete and perfect it on a higher
level of activity, that constitutes the true "principle" of
the moral life.

THE INSTRUMENTAL CAUSALITY OF THE
HUMANITY OF CHRIST

St. Thomas never ceased repeating and insisting upon
the fact that God is the principal cause and the humanity
of Christ the instrumental cause of these structures of
the supernatural life, of sanctifying grace, of the virtues,
of the gifts of the Holy Spirit. An effect as such does not
resemble the instrumental cause, but rather the principal
cause. It is in this sense that the supernatural structures
are essentially "deiform." But the instrumental cause
does intervene either to produce an effect that disposes
the recipient for the action of the principal cause, or it
just *modifies* the action of the principal cause (all this
is called *to act dispositively*). Even in this second case,
the intervention of the instrumental cause introduces into
the total effect a *modification*, which would not be there

had it not intervened. The doctrine of the instrumental causality of the humanity of Christ implies, then, of necessity, in each and every one of the supernatural life's structures—grace, the virtues, the gifts of the Holy Spirit —the presence not indeed of a change of essence, but of a real, physical modality that is in the strict sense of the term christological. Let us try to point up a few aspects or elements of this new modality.

THE TRACT ON BEATITUDE AND CHRISTOLOGY

The vision of God is the keystone of the thomistic moral theology without which this predominant "eschatological" factor must of necessity lead to neglecting the development in time of the economy of salvation.[11] What, then, is to be said of the beatific vision? It is a strange and noteworthy fact that St. Thomas, when quoting 9 times in the I Pars and in the I-II the text of *St. John* 17, 3, invariably leaves out the second part: *and whom thou hast sent, Jesus Christ.* On the contrary, in the II-II, q. 1, art. 8, which deals with the articles of the Creed, he writes: *two things are offered to us for our vision and contemplation (that is, in eternal life), namely, the hidden secrets of the divinity, the vision of which*

---

11. Cf. on this matter V. CONGAR, *Le sens de l'économie salutaire dans la théologie de Saint Thomas d'Aquin*, Festgabe J. Lortz, Baden-Baden 1958, pp. 73-122.

makes us blessed, and the mystery of the Incarnation of Christ. Then follows the quotation from *John* 17, 3, this time in full. In his commentary on this text of John (In Evang. Joannis, cap. 17, lect. 1), he teaches the same thing: *by this text we are given to understand that in life eternal the humanity of Christ will also constitute an object of our joy and delectation.* To whoever has studied the doctrine of the I Pars, q. 12, it will be clear that the humanity of Christ could not possibly constitute the "medium" of the vision of God, since this "medium" must be absolutely uncreated and be identical with the divine essence itself. Only this constitutes the formal object "quod," the vision of which renders man essentially complete in being and constitutes him in the state of ultimate felicity as a consequence, as is indeed borne out by the text which we quoted from the II-II. On the other hand, the humanity of Christ, whether in the very act itself of the vision of the divine essence, through which the divine decrees are made known to us, or by means of another quite distinct type of knowledge, *extra Verbum,* constitutes, without any doubt whatever, the second object of the beatific vision. Besides the *lumen gloriae,* the light of glory, which is indispensable for the vision of God, depends, as do grace and the virtues, on the instrumental causality of the humanity of Christ. As a result it, too, contains a christological modality, on which St. Thomas does not supply us with any details, no more than he does with regard to sanctifying grace, wth regard to which he affirms the instrumental causality of the humanity of Christ (see II-II, 112, 1 ad 2).

FIDES CHRISTI

It is above all in the tract on faith that some authors have tried to find in St. Thomas some trace of Personalism. St. Thomas was not at all aware of the "phenomenological attitude," but he did attempt to describe divine faith *on analogy* with faith in the natural order, and this he did with all due reservation, *servatis servandis*, for it is clear that divine faith implies a certitude and a firmness which are lacking altogether in human faith, by which we give credence to that told us by other human beings.

However, even in the natural order faith, on analysis, is seen to be an *ensemble* of "inter-personal" relations. Experience grasps *facts*, science or scientific knowledge adheres with certitude to a series of deductions, rigorously linked together, as was the case in euclidean geometry, the "science" *par excellence* according to the ancients. Faith, on its side, adheres or assents to the *testimony of someone.* The object of faith is not apprehended by the senses, it is not known by intellectual evidence, but it is *believed*, because a witness, who is worthy of being believed, testifies to it.[12]

That presupposes precisely, as we have just said, that the witness be *worthy of belief*, that he merit credence. We de not believe inveterate liars, nor do we believe people who are themselves too credulous, nor those who might, for one reason or another, have an evident interest in leading us astray. Human tribunals themselves pay great attention to the "morality" of the witnesses they are examining. No confidence is had in witnesses of "dubious morality," nor does one rely on those who accept too easily the gifts of those at law, of either the plaintiffs or the defendants.

This is sufficient to show that faith presupposes a judgment of value on the "person" of the witness. We believe the "testimony of good men," was a remark of St. Thomas.[13] It is necessary that they be also consciously regarded or judged as such. Faith in that way supposes and includes an act of "homage" done to the person of the witness: *credere est cortesia*, as remarked the theologian Bañez.

Divine faith, then, is first and foremost an adhering or assenting to Christ as a *witness* worthy of being believed: *assentire Christo*. Then it will appear as an assent

12. ST. THOMAS, II-II, q. 11, .a 1: Quia vero quicumque credit, alicuius dictis assentit, principale videtur esse . . . unaquaque credulitate, *ille* cuius dicto assentitur.

13. III Sent., dist. 23, q. 2, a. 2, qla 2, n° 149.

to the *truths* which he teaches us and reveals to us. It is in that way that St. Thomas explains the difference between heresy and infidelity. Heresy "chooses" between the dogmas or defined truths, pretending all the while to maintain adherence or assent to Christ; infidelity (that is, positive and not purely negative infidelity) rejects all, both Christ himself and the dogmas. In any event, the person of Christ is in that way brought very much to the fore and emphasized, and the analyses of St. Thomas are certainly not without analogy with the personalist teachings.

Let us try to make all this a little more precise. We can distinguish four elements in faith: 1) the "material" object, that namely which we believe; 2) the *act* of testimony itself, for we do not believe someone who says or testifies nothing; 3) the *person* of the withness: we believe the testimony of a person; 4) the "axiological qualities" which makes this person worthy of belief and this corresponds, grosso modo, to the formal motive, to the formal object *quo*, of the Scholastics. We will find, then, in divine faith, a *human testimony*, since Christ, true God and true man, has really spoken and revealed to us the Father in human speech, in a human testimony. But, in the strict sense of the term, we have not to do here with a *human witness*, for every witness is essentially a person, and in Christ *there is no other personality but the divine personality*. Consequently the formula used by St. Thomas, *assentire Christo*, cannot be restricted to the human testimony *alone* of Christ, but includes the divine Person of the Word Incarnate, who addressed us in human speech.

Nowadays certain theologians who wished to resurrect the ancient doctrine of the *Homo assumptus* (Deodatus of Basly, Seiler) would certainly give quite a different explanation of the structure of faith. In Christ, perfect God and perfect man, they would maintain, there are not just two natures, whole and entire, the divine nature and the human nature, but also two *subjects* of being and action, two autonomous and distinct subjects. In that case, then, the *Homo assumptus*, would be a witness distinct from the divine Word. Christ, they would say, is man, who speaks about God. In the Christology of St. Thomas, which takes its inspiration from the thought of St. Cyril and the Pseudo-Denis, Christ is God, who speaks with a human mouth, in human speech, as Gardeil used to say. From the metaphysical point of view the difference is fundamental.

It is necessary to emphasize again the following point. The theological virtues, according to the demands of their very essential structure, all have God for *object*. That means that in faith the "first motive" by which we believe, will of necessity be something essentially un-

created, the *Veracity* of God, who cannot "be deceived
or deceive," *nec falli nec fallere potest* (Conc. Vat. I,
DENZS 3008). St. Thomas expresses this teaching when
he affirms that the "first Truth" is the "formal" object of
faith.[14] It is not possible, then, to include the humanity
of Christ and the created "axiological qualities" which
it contains, in the "formal" motive of faith. But if we
leave this "reason for believing" aside and consider the
person whom we believe, it should be remarked that the
humanity of Christ, united in an ineffable manner to the
Word of the Father, *does not constitute a plurality with
the Person itself of the witness*. It is the whole and total
Christ, God and man, that gives testimony. And together with the person of the Word, it is also the Father
who is witness: *I am testifying on my own behalf but
the Father who sent me is my witness too*,[15] and the
Holy Spirit also: *He will give his evidence about me*.[16]

CHRISTIAN HOPE

St. Thomas has explained the structure of the
second theological virtue in a way that corresponds
exactly to the manner in which he explained the nature

---

14. ST. THOMAS, II-II, q. 1, a. 1.
15. John 8, 18.
16. John 15, 26.

of faith. Hope is an affective movement of "tension" towards a good that is remarkable for its greatness or desirability and also for the difficulty which we have in attaining it (*bonum arduum*). But this movement of tension presupposes and includes an act of trust in the *person*, whose help will enable us to arrive at the goal. That is precisely what St. Thomas says in his question *De spe* (art 1): *the activity of hope bears upon two objects, namely, on the good to be attained, and on HIM upon whose help reliance is placed*. Christian hope, consequently, tends towards the transcendent good of the blessed life of heaven, and that it does relying on the omnipotence and mercy of God (*auxilium divinae potestatis et pietatis*). The power and the mercy of God are in that sense our "reasons" for hoping, just as the supreme Veracity of God is our "reason" for believing. But in the last analysis one does not hope in a thing, one hopes *in someone*, in a *person*. And when it is a question of the theological hope that has God for object, then that can only be the Three divine Persons, the Father, the Son and the Holy Spirit. Does one not also hope in Christ? Or to be more precise: in the humanity of Chist? Yes, of course, for the simple reason that it is the conjoined instrument of his divinity and it is from it that come to us the divine promises that are our reason for hoping to obtain the divine help.

CHARITY

In a famous article of the "Summa Theologica" St. Thomas has defined charity as a "friendship" between man and God.[17] Giving the Aristotelian analysis of friendship and applying the result of this analysis to charity, St. Thomas concludes that queen of the virtues is essentially a mutual love between God and him whom He has adopted as his son, a love founded on an assured "communicatio" of the good of heavenly beatitude. Needless to say, this "communicatio" here below is imperfect (*in spe, non in re*); it is the future life that it will find its full perfection.

St. Thomas had previously expounded his thought on this matter more completely and more lucidly still. "He who is admitted to becoming a member of city or state must possess the moral virtues that are necessary for the carrying out of his activity as citizen. Above all it is necessary that he be filled with *love for the common good of the city or state*, that admits him amongst its members. Now man, by means of divine grace, is admitted to becoming a member of the blessed city that is called in Sacred Scripture the Heavenly Jerusalem. Admitted in that way to sharing the common good of the celestial realities, man must be henceforth in possession of new virtues, the infused virtues, the exercise of which presupposes *love for the common good of the celestial*

---

17. ST. THOMAS, II-II, q. 23, a. 1.

city, a common good that is none other than the divine Good, God himself, the object of eternal beatitude." This love of the common good, adds St. Thomas, is charity.[18]

One might say that these explanations insist above all on the *eschatological* character of charity. Already here below it is a "celestial" virtue. The temporal function of charity, its role in the life of here below, do not seem, for the moment, to hold the attention of the Angelic Doctor. For this one has to wait till the questions concerning mercy and almsgiving. Here not another thing speaks to us of Christ.

He is not absent for all that. Having pointed out that the "communicatio" of celestial beatitude is the "foundation" of the new friendship that is charity, St. Thomas adds: *concerning this "communicatio" we read in I Cor. (1, 9): the God, who has called you into the fellowship of his Son, Jesus Christ our Lord, is faithful to his promise.* The "communicatio," then, is not just the divine likeness which grace gives us, it is also an "entry into society," a *life* in society or in company with the Father, with the Son, the Word Incarnate, true God and true man, and with the Holy Spirit which they bestow upon us. As St. Thomas pointed out with such great precision in his commentary on the text quoted by him here, this life in company with God the Father, in Christ

18. Quaes. Disp. *De caritate* a. 2.

and through Christ, begins already in this life, albeit in an imperfect manner. Christ indeed found a visible society, *the Church*. The *ecclesial character* of charity, then, is seen to be virtually contained in its *social* character, which St. Thomas strongly emphasized.

Leaving out of account certain minor texts (II. II, 24, 2; 24, 8; 24, 9; 32, 6; 40, 2; 43, 5), it is in the question on schism that we meet the same thought again, christological and ecclesial at one and the same time. Charity is a spiritual bond of love that is the principle of union not only between two persons: it is also the principle of unity for the whole Church: *it unifies . . . the whole Church in the unity of the Spirit.* There follows then the very well known text: Now, if one examine the matter attentively it will be found that the unity of the Church consists in two things: on the one hand, in the union of the Church's members amongst themselves, that is to say, in a communion or community; and on the other hand, in the relation of all the Church's members to one head. . . . But this head is Christ himself, whose office in the Church is exercised by the Supreme Pontiff (II.II, q. 39, art. 1).

But this refers more to the "material" object of charity, that which is loved. What about the formal object? In the case of the theological virtues this formal object "quo" cannot be anything but God himself under a certain aspect of a determined attribute, and here it is

God as sovereign Goodness, "the object of Beatitude,"
Bonum divinum beatitudinis obiectum. Consequently it
is impossible that a created reality like the humanity of
Christ should constitute the formal motive of charity: it
is something unique and simple. But, on the other hand,
even if the divine benefits cannot be the motive of the
love of God, who must be loved for his own sake, nonetheless is the order of material and dispositive causality,
they do constitute so many different "reasons" for loving
God.

St. Thomas refused to admit the impossible dilemma:
either interested love, or disinterested love! either to love
from the motive of one's own interest (*amor mercena-
rius*), or, renouncing completely one's own interest, to
love God with "pure" love, going so far as to being disinterested even in the recompense of eternal life, to
detaching oneself from this recompense and from every
desire of the celestial fatherland. In fact, the *first* motive,
the "formal" motive of charity is God himself (*He is
loved "for his own sake"*), by reason of his infinite goodness and his infinite perfection. But, on the other hand,
the benefits either already received from God or hoped
for (eternal life) *dispose* us for the love of God, in so
far as they are an indispensable disposition, *ex parte
causae materialis*, for the love of God. Amongst these
benefits which the human race has received from God,
is not the greatest of all the Incarnation, prolonged and

continued by the mysteries of Christ's life, by sacramental action, by the teaching office and the maternal
government of the Church? In that fundamental article
in St. Thomas' tract on charity (II-II, q. 27, art. 3) we
have discovered the possibility of inserting the place of
Christ and of the Church, which can never be separated
from Christ.

And here is, perhaps, the essential point. As every
other friendship, charity is essentially a mutual love
between *persons*. The personal term of charity-friendship
is not some abstract "idea" or the "God of the philosophers." Charity is friendship with the Father, *and* with
the Son, *and* with the Holy Spirit. It reaches the persons, each separately and distinctly, according to each
person's own properties.

What place are we to assign here to the humanity
of Christ? There can be no question of making it a
fourth personal term of the movement of love: that
would be Nestorianism. This danger once set aside,
there still remain serious discussion[19] which cannot fail
to have their repercussion on the doctrine of charity. If
the human nature of Christ, while being a perfect and
an "individuated" nature, is not for all that in any way
a "subject," a "quod," an "individuum" (in the neutral),

---

19. On the present-day "tendencies" in Christology, cf. J. GALOT,
La psychologie du Christ, NRT 80, (1958) 337-358, which gives a very
clear picture of the present state of the question.

then it is clear that the movement of charity will have only one term: the person of the Logos subsisting in the two natures, the divine and the human. A moral theology that draws its inspiration from these magnificent ideas, will insist above all on the "deification" of the Christian, in relation to the *divine* nature of the Logos made Flesh, the role of the sacred humanity appearing, from this point of view, as an essentially *instrumental* one. This is the position of St. Thomas.

On the contrary, should one open the door to the doctrines of the "Homo assumptus," that the "Ego" of "Jesus" be no longer that of the Word made Flesh, but that of the "man assumed" by him, that the "Man assumed" be not indeed a person, but fully *subject, quod, individuum*, then there follows necessarily from that a certain *doubling* in the term of charity-friendship. Over and above the person of the Word, the *Homo assumptus*, after the manner of a *subject*, constitutes a distinct term of love, a term which is certainly not a person, but which is still, in its own right, truly *that which* is loved. What follows from this with reference to the structure of moral theology? This follows: that one will insist less on the "deification" of the Christian by the Word made Flesh or on the deiform character of the structures of the supernatural life and will come rather to seeing in these structures the principles of assimilation to the "Homo assumptus." In that case, will not one run the risk of immediately seeing and teaching an opposition between "Christocentrism" and "Theocentrism"?

THE MORAL VIRTUES AND CHRIST

St. Thomas frequently remarks that the theological virtues ordain us towards our end, towards the supreme goal of human life, towards God who is their object. On the contrary, the moral virtues have to do with the *means*, that is, with all that which, in the context of "temporality," of the use of terrestrial realities, should be ordained to God. One cannot be a Christian without practicing justice, patience, temperance, chastity according to the demands of one's state in life: the perfect chastity of virgins, conjugal chastity, or the chastity of widows and widowers.

In the vast tableau of virtues which he puts before us, St. Thomas adopts the plan of the cardinal virtues. All the other virtues are reduced to these, they are their various *parts*. It is precisely this "reduction" which, nowadays, causes so much difficulty for many minds and disturbs them. Why, they ask, this pre-eminence accorded to the "Greek" virtues and to pagan virtues? No one denies their existence and reality and their necessity even for the Christian life. But would it not be better to point up and emphasize more the "Christian" virtues, humility, Christian virginity and above all religion?

St. Thomas was not at all ignorant of the pre-eminent place of humility in the Christian life. Christ recommended it above everything else.[20] With regard to the cardinal virtues, and as far as the "Greek" virtues too are concerned, there is a great deal of manifest confusion here. These four virtues, prudence, justice, fortitude and temperance, are "principal" virtues, not in the sense that they are the most "perfect" virtues and the most noble ones, but precisely because they are of *common use*, of daily use in a certain sense, and every human life must put them daily into practice.

And there is something more. St. Thomas admits the existence of *infused* moral virtues, essentially and specifically distinct from the pagan and the "Greek" virtues. According to this point of view, the justice or temperance of the Christian differ essentially from the justice or temperance as described by Aristotle or the Stoics. In order to explain this distinction appeal is frequently made to the distinction and the opposition in the *motives* of action. It is pointed out, for example, that an alms can be given from the motive or intention of natural philanthropy or with a religious intention, in honor of Christ or for his sake, for instance, who suffers in his members. Such an explanation really avoids the problem. Even if it were so, then it would be easy to answer that *Charity*, the queen and the form of all the virtues, is able to ordain

20. ST. THOMAS, II-II, q. 161, a. 5 ad 4.

to God the acts of all the different moral virtues. It would in no wise be necessary to postulate the existence of *new* virtues distinct from the acquired moral virtues. This was already the argument of Duns Scotus, and it is still that of a very large number of modern theologians who follow him.

But it must be noted that, if we consider only the motive, then we remain outside the *essence* of the virtue. The alms itself and the intention or "motive" for which it is given are two quite distinct things. The intention belongs to the order of the *end,* the essence is determined by the *object.* The end, which is the proper object of intention, give to the act an *extrinsic* specification which in no way destroys its intrinsic specification but rather presupposes it. Were one to limit oneself to the consideration of motives then it will always be possible to say that faith, hope and charity suffice to ordain the whole of man's moral activity to the supernatural end.

But that is just what St. Thomas did not do, he did not base his demonstration on a consideration of motives, but rather on a consideration of the *rule*: this, the rule used by infused justice is not the same as that used by acquired justice, by the justice of the philosophers. But why then a "rule"? Natural agents, and animals, always act in the same way. They are limited *ad unum*, to one way of acting. Man, on the contrary, has before him an ocean of "possibilities." But man cannot will just anything whatever, in any place and at any time. In human actions there is *good* and *evil*, some of them being good and some bad. It is the "rule" of morality which renders possible such a discernment. That is good which is in conformity with the moral rule, and that is evil which is in opposition to it. Consequently the rule of morality imposes on the determined "matter" (for example, the pleasures attached to the use of food or sexuality) its own proper *measure*, its own modality, by which the acts are made virtuous.

St. Thomas has explained precisely what this difference of modality, this difference of "rule" is, that distinguishes the infused virtue from the corresponding acquired virtue. "The measure imposed on the movements of the sensitive appetite by the rule of human reason is *of a different nature* to that which is imposed by the *divine* rule, which is that of the infused virtues. For instance, in the use of food, the judgment of reason limits itself to forbidding whatever would harm the health of the body or impede the use of the intellectual faculties. The divine rule of the infused virtues demands more. It demands that the Christian, according to the word of St. Paul, chastise his body and bring it into subjection (*J Cor.* 9, 27) by abstinence and mortification."[21] It should be remarked that *asceticism*, unknown to the purely rational rule of morality, is not just any

21. I-II, q. 63, a. 4.

kind of ascenticism. In reality it is a question of *imitating the Cross of Christ*. That is the only way in which Christian mortification has meaning. The proper rule, then, of infused temperance is essentially a *Christian* rule in which the imitation of the Cross of Christ has the preponderant part to play.

In the same way it will be immediately evident that Christian fortitude and courage are something quite distinct from the military valor of the heroes of antiquity. In like manner, too, Christian prudence has insights, a way of judging and of directing action that distinguishes it radically from the purely "natural" considerations of acquired prudence. Let us recall here that the "prudence" of the moralists is not the same as that of the automobilists or that of business and financiers. In moral theology we are dealing with an intellectual virtue which exercises a sovereign and over-all directive action on the totality of moral activity. It is its business to *deliberate*, to *judge* with rectitude, and to bring the work to completion and to its term.[22]

---

22. For all that it is perhaps, here question rather of a *modality* than of the substance of the rule. The temperance of Adam, that of original justice, could not in fact have implied this ascetical exigence. Between that and the infused temperance of fallen and redeemed nature St. Thomas would refuse to see an essential difference. The motive, the rule of infused temperance, of the two forms of infused temperance, is, as a consequence, more exactly expressed in the formulae of the *De virtutibus* (q. 5, a. 4): *virtutes cardinales, secundum quod sunt gratuitae et infusae . . . perficiunt hominem in vita praesenti in ordine ad caelestem gloriam.* Infused temperance is the rule for the use of and the desire of pleasures of touch, in a subject that is *called to celestial*

JUSTICE

But in the case of justice a serious difficulty makes its appearance. It has to do with the absolute quality of things, of goods, in their external existence. If I owe a 100 dollars, then I owe 100 whoever the person be to whom I owe them. Justice never changes according to the spiritual character of the person who has a debt. It knows nothing but the rigor of objective right. Every distinction between a supernatural rule or "measure" and a rule of the natural order seems to vanish.

To this difficulty one can answer first of all that justice must assuredly be tempered in its rigor by the intervention of other virtues, above all by that of *liberality* (generosity) and mercy,[23] and it is an easy matter to establish the "religious" and Christian character of these virtues. In the regard it will be well to consider the parable of the unmerciful debtor.[24] The insolvent servant, who is absolved from the very large debt of 10,000 talents (about $9,000,000, a deliberately fantastic amount), had, in strict justice, the right to exact

life. But by reason of the subject in which it is found, in sinful man redeemed by Christ, infused temperance takes on a new "modality," which it would not have had in the state of original justice: and that modality is the necessity of mortification and of the imitation of the Cross of Jesus.—These reflections are inspired by the very pertinent remarks of F. UTZ, *St. Thomas, Summa Theol,* Deutsch-Lat. Ausgabe, t. 11, Salzburg-Leipzig 1940, pp. 600-601.

23. II-II, q. 58, a. 11, ad 1.
24. Matt. 18, 23-35.

from his fellow-servant the payment of the 100 denarius which he owed him. But because he on his part did not also use mercy he is severely condemned.

But what about justice in itself? And first of all what about *legal* justice? It pertains to it to refer or ordain to the common good of the political city, of the state, the acts of all the other virtues. Aristotle put this virtue in the very highest place. Much superior to the cardinal virtue of justice it shines in the firmament of the virtues like the "morning star." The Christian can appreciate the greatness and splendor of this noble virtue. But he knows, too, that above and superior to political society there is another city, the Church, and he knows that the role of supreme virtue assigned by Aristotle to legal justice, is the prerogative not of another virtue, of *charity*.[25] If the Christian state is different from the pagan state, if the Christian citizen is not to be identified with the citizen of the ancient world, then one should no longer be surprised to find that the legal justice of the Christian is different from the legal justice which Aristotle described so magnificently. It no longer considers the State to be the supreme value, and subordinates it to higher values.

As far as *distributive* justice, a part of the cardinal virtue of justice, is concerned, it must take "persons" into account. In fact, it is the business of this form of justice

---

25. Quaest. Disp. *De oar.*, a. 2.

to portion out between several an amount of goods, of
recompenses, of helps, and of offices too, even of taxes
to be paid. There is no place here for mathematical
equality, which would take no account of the status of
these different persons. On the contrary, it is imperative
that he, who is charged with this apportioning, take
the greatest possible care to establish a *proportion* between that which he is to distribute to each one and
this one's importance in reference to the common good:
*the more important person's position in the community,
the greater share is given him of the community's common goods.*[26] Aristotle already made the remark that
different political regimes—monarchy, aristocracy, de-
mocracy—each attribute a different value to persons.
That is to say, that distributive justice presupposes a
"judgment of value" on the *persons,* a judgment which
will be its rule and its measure. One can consequently
surmise that *infused* distributive justice, which takes into
account *Christian* persons, will pass a different judgment
on them than that of purely natural justice.

There remains to be considered now the more dif-
ficult case of *commutative* justice. Here it is not a question at all of establishing a proportion between goods
and persons, but of establishing an *equality* between one
good (understood in the sense of political economy,

---

26. II-II, q. 61, a. 2.

namely, that which is capable of satisfying any need of human life) and another good, another thing. I have received 100 and I owe 100. The transaction seems to take on the same mathematical rigor as the calculation of the distance between two planets in the solar system. In reality things are not as simple as all that. The exchange of goods takes place between *men*, the goods are no more than the *instruments* of social relations. In the contract of buying and selling, for instance, it is a question of giving the "just price" for the thing one wishes to acquire. The just price corresponds to the *value* (in the economic sense of the term). But the value of the thing is not determined by its nature, as is the distance from one point to another. It depends on common "estimate," on the judgment of the men of a particular time and of a particular country. But what is the origin of this common estimate? The ancients already had an answer to this question: from the *utility* or *usefulness* of the things, that is, from its greater or lesser capacity to meet the need of human life. Traditional political economy adds another element to this: *rarity* or *scarcity* (what is rare is dear, is a saying of sound common sense). Modern science, with its theory of marginal utility, has made more perfect and precise these popular observations and convictions, while Marxism seeks the principle of economic value in the quality of *human labor* that has been incorporated into the thing. In any event, man has been brought in again as the measure of relations in the whole economic system.

Modern jurists, for their part, maintain that commutative justice, as well as every other form of justice, presupposes the "recognition of the value of persons."[27] A human being, a person, does not regard himself as under an obligation to a *thing*, but to another person. This "recognition of the value of the person" is not very evident in the many operations of commutative justice which we carry out every day, in our daily acquisitions. But let us take, for example, the obligations of retribution and indemnification that arise from homicide, even involuntary homicide. These obligations are regulated by the axiological qualities of the person who has been the victim of such an injustice. Let us suppose that the injury has been done to a person consecrated to God, then, precisely on account of his consecration we will have a new species of injustice, *sacrilege* namely, which is understandable only in reference to infused justice. And here is another example: that which we call the labor contract, the *locatio operum* of the ancient jurists, is inconceivable with considering the persons of the employer and employee. The relations between *Christian* employers and laborers cannot be considered as identical with those that might be put forward by a purely natural

27. G. DEL VECCHIO, *La giustizia*, Rome 1946, p. 66, n. 7.

justice. This will suffice to show that it is not impossible to discover in the domain of justice the double rule and the double measure that enables us to distinguish the acquired virtue from the infused.

THE GIFTS OF THE HOLY SPIRIT

It was above all with regard to the gifts of the Holy Spirit that the theologian of the Middle Ages developed and expounded the theme of the imitation of Christ.[28] With reference precisely to this St. Thomas criticized the doctrine of Philip the Chancellor, who saw in the virtues the principles of good works, whereas through the gifts we become like to Christ, in a special way through the imitation of his Passion. St. Thomas did not in any way exclude this last idea, but he adds that the virtues also make us like to Christ and are so many different principles of the imitation of Christ. For, before everything else, Christ teaches us, in his Passion, *gentleness, humility* and *charity*, virtues of which he is for us the incomparable model. Now, humility and meekness are *virtues*, and not gifts of the Holy Spirit. We already mentioned above this important text which concerns—that goes without saying—the infused, not the acquired, virtues.

---

28. The very rich doctrine of St. Bonaventure is to be found, for example, in: III Sent., dist. 11, 1; dist. 28, a. 1, q. 3, fund. 4; dist. 15, a. 1, q. 1.

Conclusion

Whereas there is only *one* Christian moral teaching, only *one* revealed morality, there is nothing against there being *several* "moral theologies," each distinct in its methods, in the immediated purpose in view, or in the different public for which it is destined. In the Middle Ages, as we saw, we can easily distinguish two moral theologies: the one, that of the "schools," of the universities aiming at the scientific analysis and deeper penetration of all the notions involved and constituting one single science with dogmatic theology; the other, that of the *Summulae* destined for the immediate use of the confessors. With the addition of the treatises on human acts, conscience and law this eventually developed into being our modern "moral theology," a science quite distinct from that of dogmatic theology. In the 19th century a new moral theology makes its appearance in Germany, a moral theology that purports to be more "Christian," more biblical and more spiritual. This new moral theology is dominated by the concept of "vitalism" (that is the action of the Spirit) and by the notion of

"Idea," the dynamic principle of growth and development, which is in no wise merely an insight or projection of the human intelligence, but rather the expression of objective reality itself. In that way moral theology becomes the history of the "Kingdom of God" progressively growing and developing. It is in the development and continuation of these notions that the moral theology of the "Imitation of Christ," brilliantly ushered in more than a quarter of a century ago now, finds its proper place.

But it is an undeniable fact that this moral theology of the "Imitation" was influenced profoundly by the personalist philosophy of Max Scheler then very much in vogue. Every man has a *"Vorbild,"* a person whom he intends to follow in the role of "disciple." The "person-model" will, in that way, be the source and the exemplar of his own moral life, of his "own scale of values" for the moral subject. That is, by and large, the position of Scheler.

It is this "principle of personal exemplarity," the primal source of all morality, that must above all be subject to examination and criticism. Does this principle have the absolute character which Scheler attributes to it and shouldn't one take into account the criticisms of N. Hartmann? It is absolutely true that man is not being completely isolated in the universe, a kind of monad shut up in itself. Round about him man finds *the others*, like himself, other persons, that is so many different models from which he draws inspiration or which he rejects. But it must also be maintained with St. Thomas that the starting point of morality, its "principle," when man arrives at the use of reason, is the apprehension of moral *good* and, more concretely, a certain knowledge of the *principles of the Natural Law*. Needless to say, the Natural Law could have no meaning for Scheler or for any other philosophy that denies the existence of a "human nature."

Let us get away now from the order of natural morality and pass on to consider the order of supernatural and revealed morality. It is clear that, for St. Thomas, the first is in no way eliminated by the latter: for grace perfects nature and does not destroy it at all. On this plane of supernatural morality there is something fundamentally exact in the ethics of personal exemplarity. St. Thomas writes that the very first conversion of man to God is through faith: *man's first turning to God is brought about through faith* (I-II, q. 113, art. 4). Now, faith is essentially the adhering of the mind to the testimony of a person, and in the case of divine faith, it is an adhering to Christ, to the person of Christ, God and Man.

What then about moral theology and its "integration" into Christology? This could be understood in a quite unorthodox sense and this must be set aside. Consequently it will be much rather a question of a linking up, of a *co-ordination*, not of an absorbing of moral theology into Christology.

Here there is a solution that is in a certain sense, to put it this way, with handreach. For the whole thomistic tradition (and indeed for St. Thomas himself), *the sacramental characters* constitute so many different formal participations in the priesthood of Christ, in the mysteries of Christ's life; they are so many different principles of formal assimilation to Christ. A moral theology, then, purporting to be fully christological, would have to link up the *ensemble* of its developments or elaborations to the *economy of the sacramental characters*, and to these it would be an easy matter to join up the other sacraments and the whole of the moral life.

Needless to say, this is not the choice of St. Thomas. Instead of linking up his moral theology to the sacramental characters and through these, in short, to Christology, he attached it, by means of the notion of "image," to the perspectives of the treatise on divine government and to the profound teaching of the tract on God, One and Three. Why this choice? It is easy to understand the reason for it. St. Thomas undertook to "thematize" the structures of the supernatural moral life, grace, the virtues, the gifts of the Holy Spirit. Now, these structures are essentially "deiform," that is, in the same way that our grace is a sharing in the fullness of created grace, in the captial grace of Christ and a participation in the *Deitas.*

Is one to conclude, then, that Christ as man is *absent* from the moral theology of St. Thomas? Certainly not! And in this respect it is not sufficient just to draw up a list of texts in which his Name is explicitly mentioned. One must take into account the defferent doctrines of St. Thomas. Christ is *everywhere present in the moral teaching of St. Thomas,* because the sacred humanity of Christ and the mysteries of his life, exercise a *universal intrumental causality* on each and every one of the structures of the supernatural life. Through this instrumental efficient causality Christ produces in these structures, in grace, the virtues, the gifts, the light of glory (*lumen gloriae*), a specifically christological modality, on which St. Thomas expatiates little and offers few details, except in the case of the infused moral virtues and the gifts of the Holy Spirit. But we know that the theology of faith as found in the work of St. Thomas has an undeniably christological structure, a structure which can be discovered without much ado in the tract on hope. In charity, friendship with God, even there, we succeeded in discovering and finding a place for the humanity of Christ.

Exemplarism, in the philsophy of St. Thomas, corresponds to that which is called the "extrinsic" formal cause. If Christ is universal physical instrumental cause, if, through his action and influence, he imprints a special "modality" on all the structures of the supernatural life, then no one should be surprised to hear St. Thomas affirm that the humanity of Christ and the mysteries of his life are a constant and universal model for Chrisians, a perfect model of life for them. For the Christian has no other way of imitating God except by imitating Christ.

In the III Pars, in the treatise on the mysteries of Christ's life, St. Thomas pointed out many times the elements of this exemplarism, taking up again in detail the synthetic vision of chapter 54 of the fourth book of the *Contra Gentiles*. Perhaps one could say that there are *two* moral theologies in the *Summa Theologica*: the one, the vast moral theology of the I-II and II-II, aimed at describing and analysing the formal structures of the supernatural life; the other, the one that is integrated into the III Pars and proposed to us these same structures in the living model which should illumine our behavior and give us the strength and courage to strive after the sublime ideal of the Christian life. But it is clear that for St. Thomas the second presupposes the first: how are we to see in Christ the ever-valid and inimitable model of our patience, of our humility and of our charity, if we do not know what are patience, humility and charity?

Consequently a moral teaching developed in funtion of "preaching" and purporting to be of thomistic inspiration would find in this "second" moral theology the elements, the "themes" of its elaborations. It would limit itself to gathering the *results* of the analyses which the I-II and the II-II have to offer us, without retaining at all the complex scientific apparatus which we find there. No one would stop such a moral theology from insisting on the Christian virtues, humility, patience, charity, religion rather than on the "Greek" virtues which today on the part of some provoke such indignation and hostility. And for all that it will enter the head of no one that the Christian be dispensed from practicing justice, courage and temperance. The "cardinal" virtues cannot be ignored so easily.

In short, the moral theology of preachers, that of confessors and scientific moral theology can *co-exist* in perfect harmony, each in its own domain. But what is to be said about this last one? Will a scientific moral theology be obliged to break loose from "Scholasticism" in order to follow in the train of the philosophy in vogue? Yesterday Blondel or Scheler, today existentialism, tomorrow, who knows what? It is very doubtful that it succeed.

GLOSSARY

Aufklarung: This technical German expression might be rendered into English by "Enlightenment," and it is used for a whole and complex movement of thought that first made its appearance in 18th century Germany. A rationalistic conception of God, creation, man and all reality is its fundamental characteristic, and this soon manifested itself in a radical opposition to and rejection of all **supernatural** religion and belief and in a desire to promote the good and pleasure of man in this life as reason left to itself could determine. The notion of sin or corruption in nature (which reason could not remedy) was completely foreign to it. It gave rise, in the course of the 19th century, to a whole movement of biblical criticism amongst the liberal Protestants, for it undermined all belief in the authority of the Bible. And at the same time it is at the root of emotional Pietism of all kinds. It also affected Catholic theology and was the cause of a die-hard antagonism to the celibacy of the clergy, and very many popular devotions of piety ([devotion to saints, pilgrimages etc.] See chapter 2, beginning).

Formgeschichte: The German expression is most frequently used, but sometimes it is englished as "form-criticism." It is a method of biblical criticism, which has its remote origins in the **Aufklarung,** and consists in trying to get to the source and thus determine the meaning of the Bible in general or of particular passages and books of it by an exact examination of their structural (literary and historical) **forms** (See chapter 4, note 23).

Nachfolge: Sometimes this word is translated by **imitation,** and as will be clear from what has been said in chapters 3 and 4, the full meaning of the original Latin expression **imitatio**

would surely justify this. However in modern English and in German **imitation** (Germ. **Nachahmung**) has a much weaker meaning and may even at times be used in a pejorative sense (mere material mimicry, etc.), and for that reason German writers are most careful to translate "imitatio Christi" by "**Nachfolge Christi.**" There is all the distinction between imitating materially Christ and **following in his footsteps**, living according to his mind and in his spirit. Although for St. Thomas the Latin **imitatio** still retained its full and pregnant meaning, he for all that speaks most frequently about Christian perfection consisting in **sequela Christi** ([for instance, II. II, 188, 7] passive).

Sein zum Tode: This is a well-known expression taken from heideggerian philosophy. And in Heidegger it must be understood in its full phenemonological setting. In pursuance of Husserl's ideas, it means the "time-conditioned" character of all things in the "world of living things" (**Lebenswelt**), and consequently their ineluctable "being-ordered" to ceasing to be, their radical incapacity to "be" **tout court** (See chapter 5, note 5).

Vernunftethik: This expression can refer to a natural moral teaching independent of divine revelation and based on a rational analysis of man's nature and its fundamental urges and needs in conformity with its rational structure. Sailer used the equivalent expression, **Moral der Vernunft,** to show that revealed moral teaching and moral theology has a sound rational basis and thus meeting the demands of the Aufklarung half-way he sought to incorporate into Christian moral teaching whatever valid and new elements he found there. In his Manual he drew up a list of 32 propositions (See chapter 2, note 13) which he deemed to pertain to the sphere of rational moral teaching (See chapter 1 and 2).

Vorbild: This word might be translated by "model" or "pattern," but in the context of Scheler's teaching and personalist philosophy it would be better rendered by "setter of example" destined to attract and to be followed according to the spirit and not in material imitation. In that sense a **Vorbild** does not lead or direct, but rather seeks to appeal by example and to attract. Hence the title of Scheler's well-known book: **Vorbilder und Fuhrer,** that is, "Setters of example," that intend that others should do as they do, and "Leaders" or "Rulers," whose intention it is that others should do as they say and command (passive).

Ziel, Zweck: Both these terms might be translated by "end," and thus be regarded as synonymous. However, **Ziel** has in fact a much wider connotation than **Zweck,** just as **imitation** (imitatio, Nachahmung) has a much wider meaning than **following** (sequela, Nachfolge). Hence one will more exactly render **Ziel** by **end, destination** or **target,** but **Zweck** by **purpose** or **design** (See chapter 2, note 39).